TOEFL® Junior™

语言形式与含义

Language Form and Meaning

刘晓琪 编著·

浙江教育出版社·杭州

图书在版编目(CIP)数据

TOEFL Junior语言形式与含义 / 刘晓琪编著. -- 杭州：浙江教育出版社，2016.7（2022.4重印）
ISBN 978-7-5536-3433-3

Ⅰ．①T… Ⅱ．①刘… Ⅲ．①TOEFL—自学参考资料
Ⅳ．①H310.41

中国版本图书馆CIP数据核字（2015）第176460号

TOEFL Junior语言形式与含义
TOEFL Junior YUYAN XINGSHI YU HANYI
刘晓琪　编著

责任编辑	赵清刚
美术编辑	韩　波
责任校对	马立改
责任印务	时小娟
装帧设计	大愚设计
出版发行	浙江教育出版社
	地址：杭州市天目山路40号
	邮编：310013
	电话：（0571）85170300 - 80928
	邮箱：dywh@xdf.cn
印　　刷	三河市良远印务有限公司
开　　本	889mm×1194mm　1/16
成品尺寸	210mm×275mm
印　　张	9.75
字　　数	184 000
版　　次	2016年7月第1版
印　　次	2022年4月第14次印刷
标准书号	ISBN 978-7-5536-3433-3
定　　价	45.00元

Preface
（前 言）

　　TOEFL Junior 考试由美国教育考试服务中心（Educational Testing Service，简称 ETS）研发推广，是"托福"家族新成员。TOEFL Junior 考试是面向英语为非母语国家的 11~15 岁中学生的国际标准化语言测试，它提供的语言成绩不仅可以帮助考生申请美国中学，也可以成为考生进一步学习英语的指南。自 2010 年 TOEFL Junior 考试开始推广以来，已经有越来越多的美国中学了解和认可这项考试，并接受其成绩作为入学语言成绩。

　　TOEFL Junior 考试于 2011 年 10 月正式进入中国，国内报考人数日益增多，考生对于考试相关信息和资料的需求亟待满足。我们以《TOEFL Junior 考试官方指南》为指导，以北美优秀教辅书为参考，结合考生参加历次考试的反馈和教师的授课、教研经验编写了这套 TOEFL Junior 辅导书，包括《TOEFL Junior 词汇精讲精练》《TOEFL Junior 语言形式与含义》《TOEFL Junior 听力》《TOEFL Junior 阅读》及《TOEFL Junior 全真模考题精讲精练》。作为 TOEFL Junior 备考辅导书籍，这套图书具有相当的实用性，适合参加 TOEFL Junior 考试的所有考生使用。

　　本书为《TOEFL Junior 语言形式与含义》，主要由三个部分组成，分别为 Vocabulary（词汇）、Grammar（语法）及 Practice（练习）。全书共 12 章。

Vocabulary：Chapter 1 到 Chapter 6 分别介绍了不同词性的词汇及其在考试中考查的知识点，后面紧跟相关的针对性练习，练习形式包括选词成句、句子填空、句子改错等。

Grammar：Chapter 7 到 Chapter 10 分别介绍了 TOEFL Junior 考题中涉及的知识点和语言点，后附练习，练习形式包括造句、翻译、句子改错等。

Practice：Chapter 11 和 Chapter 12 提供了大量练习题供考生强化训练。其中，Chapter 11 包含 6 套小型模拟练习题，供考生平时练习使用。Chapter 12 包含 2 套题目，从题目设置和题量上模拟 TOEFL Junior 考试，供考生在考前模拟练习使用。

最后，非常感谢关心和支持本书出版的新东方大愚文化传播有限公司和本书的教研团队，是他们的努力才使本书得以顺利出版。

祝愿所有考生在本书的帮助下都能够顺利地通过 TOEFL Junior 考试。

编　者

Contents
（目　录）

Grammar（语法）

Practice（练习）

General Introduction to TOEFL® Junior™ Test
（TOEFL® Junior™ 考试简介）

    TOEFL® Junior ™考试是美国教育考试服务中心 (ETS) 专门针对 11~15 岁中学生研究设计的一项英语能力水平测试。考试旨在衡量中学生在校园学术生活和日常社会生活中的英语语言水平，能够反映学生在以英语为媒介的教学环境中的英语能力。TOEFL® Junior ™考试不仅为准备出国留学的中学生提供了一项权威的语言证明，而且能够准确、全面地反映出所有考生前一阶段学习的进步状况，并且为后一阶段的继续学习提供具有参考价值的指导。

    TOEFL® Junior ™考试是一项精心设计的考试，它能够客观评估学生的英语水平，并为教师和家长提供有关学生英语水平和能力的有用信息。为了帮助学生（尤其是中学生）衡量自己的英语能力，TOEFL® Junior ™的成绩可分别与美国中学生英语水平对比体系 (Grade Levels in the United States)、蓝思阅读分级体系 (Lexile Reader Measure)、欧洲语言共同框架 (Common European Framework of Reference for Languages) 三个可信赖的测评体系相对接，以衡量考生的英语能力。

    TOEFL® Junior ™考试共分为三部分：听力理解 (Listening Comprehension)、语言形式与含义 (Language Form and Meaning) 和阅读理解 (Reading Comprehension)。 每部分包含 42 道单项选择题，共 126 题；每部分满分 300 分，总分为 900 分。考试采用纸笔考试和机考两种形式，总时长为 115 分钟。

科目	考试时间	分数范围
听力理解	40 分钟	200~300 分
语言形式与含义	25 分钟	200~300 分
阅读理解	50 分钟	200~300 分
总计	115 分钟	600~900 分

Language Form and Meaning Overview
（语言形式与含义概述）

    TOEFL® Junior ™考试中的语言形式与含义部分共由 6 至 8 篇小短文组成，每篇小短文对应 4 至 8 道题目。该部分总共有 42 道题，全部为单项选择题。考试时间为 25 分钟。

    该部分包括两大类型，分别为语言形式 (Language Form) 和语言含义 (Language Meaning)。这两大类型会以便条、邮件、公告等形式，或以学生习作、课文、杂志中节选出的较为学术的文章的形式出现。题目内容贴近校园生活，是考生日常生活常见、常用的题材形式。

1. 题目形式

形式		题目数量	考试时间
篇幅较短 （4 至 5 句话）	信件	0~2 道	25 分钟
	通知、公告	0~2 道	
	记叙文	1~2 道	
篇幅较长 （8 至 10 句话）	学生习作	0~3 道	
	课文节选	0~2 道	
	杂志文章	0~2 道	

2. 考查内容类型

类型	考查内容	题目数量
语言形式 （占 65% 题目）	动词	24~32 道
	比较	
	固定搭配	
	从句	
	句型结构	
语言含义 （占 35% 题目）	词汇选择	10~18 道

Sample Questions
（样题）

Questions 1~4 refer to the following e-mail.

Hi, Linda!

Thanks for your last e-mail! I know you like art, just like I do, so I wanted

1.
(A) tell
(B) told
(C) to tell
(D) telling

you about the special trip my class went on last week. We took

2.
a bus into the city and spent two hours at the art museum,

(A) if there was
(B) that there was
(C) which we had
(D) where we had

our own tour guide. The guide told us about the different artists and gave us the

3.
history of some of the paintings.

(A) When
(B) Rather
(C) During
(D) Whether

I have more time, I will send

you another e-mail with some of the photos I took that day. I took a lot of them! If

4.
your family comes to

(A) ask
(B) visit
(C) look
(D) return

us this year, we can go to the art museum

together.

Your cousin,

Samantha

Questions 5~12 refer to the following magazine article.

5.　Located in central Africa,

(A)　Lake Victoria is
(B)　and Lake Victoria is
(C)　Lake Victoria's being
(D)　although Lake Victoria is

a very unusual lake.

6.

(A) It not only one is
(B) Is it one not only
(C) One is it only not
(D) Not only is it one

of the largest lakes in the world; it is also one of the

youngest. Estimated to be about 15,000 years old, it is a relative baby compared

7.　with Earth's other very large lakes,

(A)　are
(B)　they are
(C)　which being
(D)　which can be

more than two million

8.　years old. Yet judging by the variety of life in it, Lake Victoria

(A)　resembles
(B)　portrays
(C)　views
(D)　likes

a much older body of water. Usually, lakes need a longer time

9.

(A)　is populated
(B)　they are populated
(C)　to become populated
(D)　becoming populating

by a diverse array of life-forms.

10.

(A)　Is
(B)　It is
(C)　Being
(D)　Because it is

common for new lakes to contain only a small number of

11. species. Lake Victoria, however, is

(A) opened
(B) packed
(C) satisfied
(D) purchased

with colorful fish, most

12. notably, cichlids. There are

(A) many
(B) as many
(C) too many
(D) as many as

500 different species of just

this one type of fish.

Answers & Explanations

1. C 本题考查 want to do sth. 的搭配。

2. D 选项前的半句话为完整句子，前后两句不涉及条件关系，所以可以判断逗号后面为非限定性定语从句，排除选项 A。非限定性定语从句不能用 that 引导，排除选项 B。句中强调的是我们的导游在 art museum 里，要用 in which，in which = where。

3. A 此句可以理解为我一有时间就会发送给你另外的邮件。rather 表示"相当"的意思；during 表示"在……期间"的意思；whether 表示"是否，不论"的意思。

4. B 句子所要表达的是"如果你们家还来 _____ 我家的话，我们可以一起去艺术博物馆"。可以判断出选项所要表达的意思是"拜访"，所以选 visit。

5. A Located in central Africa 为句子插入语，可以先忽略不看，通过选项内容加后面的 a very unusual lake 构成句子"主系表"结构，符合要求的只有选项 A。

6. D "；"连接两个句子构成平行结构。后边是 it is also one of...，前边应对称为 it is not only one of...，表示它"不仅是……还是……"，选项 A、B 和 C 表达错误，可排除。选项 D 为倒装句式，not only 在句首时，第一个分句的主语和谓语部分需要颠倒位置。

7. D Estimated to be about 15,000 years old 为插入语，可以先忽略。后面半句 it is a relative baby compared with Earth's other very large lakes，后面半句"主系表"结构已经齐全，说明选项之后引导的是非限定性定语从句（通常有逗号间隔的为非限定性），用来补充说明 Earth's other very large lakes，故本题只可以选择 which 引导，being 不能作谓语动词。

8. A 此题容易受生词的影响。句子需要表达的是"类似，相像"的意思。resembles 表示"像，类似于"的意思；portrays 表示"描写，描绘；扮演，饰演"的意思；views 表示"看待，考虑，把……视为"的意思；likes 虽然有"像，如同"的意思，但不作动词，而是作介词或连词使用，可直接排除。

9. C need 表示"需要"的意思时，使用固定搭配 need to do sth.。

10. B 做题时可直接排除选项 A 和 C，因为两者不符合句子的构成要素。由于下一句出现 however，所以不存在因果关系，可排除选项 D。

11. B 句子要表示的是 Lake Victoria 里有很多五颜六色的鱼。opened 表示"开放"的意思；packed 表示"充满"的意思；satisfied 表示"满意"的意思；purchased 表示"购买"的意思。根据题意，正确选项为 packed。

12. D there be 句型表示"某处有某物"，句子可以被理解为"这里的一种鱼类（cichlids）有 500 个不同的品种"。"A... + as/so + 形容词原级 + as + B"，表示 A 与 B 在某方面程度相同或不同。

Vocabulary

（词 汇）

Chapter 01

Verb
（动词）

Diagnostic Test

1. — How about the exhibition yesterday?
   — It was very noisy, but that didn't _____ me.
   A. impress
   B. hurt
   C. change
   D. bother

2. — How about going hiking this weekend?
   — Sorry. I prefer _____ rather than _____.
   A. to go out; stay at home
   B. to stay at home; go out
   C. staying at home; to go out
   D. going out; stay at home

3. World Expo 2010 Shanghai China _____ people from all over the world to the theme "Better City, Better Life".
   A. attends
   B. attracts
   C. allows
   D. advises

4. The young man used to _____ to work, but he is used to _____ to work now.
   A. drive; walking
   B. drove; walked
   C. drive; walks
   D. driving; walk

5. — Look! There is a tall tree over there. Can you _____, Dave?

   — Yes, let me _____ a try.

   A. fall it off; make

   B. send it up; to have

   C. come it down; give

   D. climb it up; have

6. — It's raining, Daisy. Please _____ an umbrella with you.

   — Thanks. I'll return it to you when I _____ back next week.

   A. take; come

   B. take; will come

   C. bring; come

   D. bring; will come

7. —The Summer Palace is wonderful. Have you ever visited any other interesting places?

   —Yes. Also, we _____ to the Great Wall.

   A. have gone

   B. have been

   C. had gone

   D. had been

8. I first met Lisa three years ago when we _____ at a radio station together.

   A. have worked

   B. had been working

   C. were working

   D. had worked

9. — I'm afraid no one will agree _____ you.

   — I don't think it _____.

   A. with; minds

   B. with; matters

   C. on; works

   D. in; trouble

10. When you _____ at the door, I _____TV with my parents.

    A. knocked; watched

    B. was knocking; watched

C. knocked; was watching

D. knock; am watching

11. **Please _____ Miss Li that we _____ able to finish the work on time.**
    A. tell; will be
    B. tells; would be
    C. told; will be
    D. told; would be

12. **It _____ ten years since my brother _____ an English teacher.**
    A. was; become
    B. was; have become
    C. has; have become
    D. has been; became

13. **— The girl _____ all her savings to the people in the Southwest for the serious drought.**
    — What a donation and what a nice girl!
    A. handed out
    B. put out
    C. sold out
    D. gave out

14. **You shouldn't _____ your hope. Everything will be better.**
    A. give up
    B. fix up
    C. cheer up
    D. put up

15. **There _____ a magic show on the school playground if it _____ next Monday afternoon.**
    A. will have; doesn't rain
    B. will have; won't rain
    C. will be; doesn't rain
    D. will be; is not raining

Knowledge Points

1. 动词的分类

在 TOEFL® Junior ™的备考和练习中，考生需要了解以下两种动词的分类：

- 及物动词 Transitive Verb 和不及物动词 Intransitive Verb

  及物动词和不及物动词的差别在于动词后面是否带有宾语。及物动词又称他动词，所表示的动作常涉及动作者以外的事物，如"吃""穿""读""写"等。及物动词后必须带有动作的对象（即宾语）。

  不及物动词后不能直接带有动作的对象（即宾语）。若要加宾语，必须先在其后添加某个介词，如 to，of，at，然后可加上宾语。不及物动词没有被动形式。

  此外，有部分动词既可以是及物动词，也可以是不及物动词。意义可能会根据情境发生一定变化，这就需要考生注意观察并理解。

- 谓语动词 Predicative Verb 和非谓语动词 Non-predicative Verb

  谓语动词指在句子中充当谓语的动词，有行为动词（及物动词和不及物动词）、系动词（be 动词）、情态动词 (must，can，could，may，might...) 和助动词 (should，will，would...) 等几种。非谓语动词可以充当主语、宾语、状语等，但不能作句子的谓语成分。非谓语动词包括动词不定式 (to do)、动名词（动词的 ing 形式）和分词（现在分词和过去分词）。

2. 动词的时态

动词时态有很多种（见下表）。在备考和练习中，考生可重点关注动词的一般现在时 (Simple Present Tense)、一般过去时 (Simple Past Tense)、一般将来时 (Simple Future Tense)、过去将来时 (Past Future Tense)、过去进行时 (Past Present Tense)、现在完成时 (Present Perfect Tense)、过去完成时 (Past Perfect Tense)、现在完成进行时 (Present Perfect Progressive Tense) 和过去完成进行时 (Past Perfect Progressive Tense) 等。

以 write 为例，该动词的各种时态构成如下：

时态种类	时态构成
一般现在时	write (writes)
一般过去时	wrote
一般将来时	will (shall) write
过去将来时	should (would) write
现在进行时	be (am, is, are) writing
过去进行时	be (was, were) writing
将来进行时	will (shall) be writing

时态种类	时态构成
过去将来进行时	should (would) be writing
现在完成时	have (has) written
过去完成时	had written
将来完成时	will (shall) have written
过去将来完成时	should (would) have written
现在完成进行时	have (has) been writing
过去完成进行时	had been writing
将来完成进行时	will (shall) have been writing
过去将来完成进行时	should (would) have been writing

3. 动词的被动语态

动词的被动语态表示主语是动作的承受者。主要用于下列几种情况：①不知道动作的执行者；②没有必要指出动作的执行者；③需要强调或突出动作的承受者；④句子的主语是动作的承受者。要将主动语态变为被动语态，一般情况下，需要首先将主动句中的宾语变为被动句中的主语，再将主动句中的主语变成被动句中的宾语，并由 by 引导。变换过程中，要注意宾格与主格的调换问题以及谓语动词要变成相应的被动形式。不及物动词不用被动语态。

在 TOEFL® Junior ™的备考和练习过程中，考生可重点关注动词的一般现在时、一般过去时、一般将来时、现在完成时、过去完成时及进行时态下的被动语态。

以 tell 为例，其被动语态的构成如下：

时态种类	被动语态
一般现在时	be (am, is, are) told
一般过去时	be (was, were) told
现在进行时	be (am, is, are) being told
现在完成时	have (has) been told
一般将来时	shall (will) be told
过去进行时	be (was, were) being told
过去完成时	had been told
过去将来时	should (would) be told
含有情态动词	can (may, must) be told

4. 非谓语动词的特殊使用方法及搭配

● 不定式 (Infinite Mood)，基本形式为：to do

不定式作主语时，常用 it 作形式主语，而将真正的主语放在句末。其结构为：It + be + adj. + (for/of sb.) to do sth.

一些谓语动词后只能用不定式作宾语，这类词常常是表示命令、打算或希望的，如：would like，like，want，wish，hope，decide，plan，expect 等等。在 find 和 think 后接不定式作宾语时，常用 it 代替，而将真正的宾语放在句末。

常见的一些不带 to 的动词不定式有：

Why not do...

Why don't you do...

Had better (not) do...

Would rather do...

Could/Would/Will you please (not) do...

此外，不定式常和疑问词 what，which，when，where，how 连用，相当于一个宾语从句。

● 动名词 (Gerund)，基本形式为：doing

动名词可作主语，谓语动词要用单数形式；

e.g. Reading is really interesting.（读书非常有趣。）

动名词可作宾语，表示一般的习惯或抽象行为或经常性的动作；

e.g. They went on walking and never stopped talking.（他们继续走，说个不停。）

动名词可作表语，且可转换成主语；

e.g. Your task is cleaning the windows./Cleaning the windows is your task.（你的任务是擦窗户。）

动名词可作定语，只表明它所修饰的词的用途或所属关系等。置于所修饰词之前。

e.g. a washing machine = a machine which is used for washing（洗衣机）

英语中有一些词后面常跟动名词，例如 finish，enjoy，mind，miss，be worth，be busy，practice，have fun，have trouble/problem in，spend...in，feel like，be used to，give up，keep on，consider，suggest，can't help 等等。

● 分词 (Participle)，基本形式包括：现在分词 -ing 和过去分词 -ed

分词可作表语，兼形容词的形式；

e.g. That book was rather boring.（那本书相当无聊。）

We were so bored that we couldn't help yawning.

（我们如此无聊以至于都忍不住打哈欠。）

分词可作定语，还可以放在名词的前面修饰名词，相当于一个定语从句；

e.g. I found him a charming person.（我发现他是一个很有魅力的人。）

The teacher gave us a satisfied smile.（老师给了我们一个满意的微笑。）

分词可作状语，表示一个同时发生的或伴随的动作；

e.g. Opening the drawer, he took out a box. （他打开抽屉，拿出了一个盒子。）

They came in, followed by some children. （他们进来了，后面跟着几个孩子。）

分词可作宾语补足语，在特定动词后使用现在分词或过去分词。

e.g. I smelt something burning. （我闻到了有东西烧着的味道。）

When they got back home, they found the room robbed.

（当他们回到家时，发现家中被盗了。）

● 不同的搭配方式表示的意思不同，这点考生可加以注意并总结积累。

例如：forget to do 表示"忘记去做某事"；forget doing 表示"忘记做了某事"。

5. 共享相同词根、词缀的单词

一个单词可由前缀 + 词根 + 后缀组成。词根可以是表示实际意义的词，前缀与后缀通常不能单独用作单词，只能附加在实义词上表示一定意义，前缀多用来限定单词的功能与方向，后缀多用来引导词性。TOEFL® Junior ™考试中会出现针对共享相同词根或词缀的单词的选择题。考生可在能力范围内对常见词根、词缀进行大量积累记忆。

Assignment & Exercise

● 句子填空：选用括号里的词的正确形式完成句子

1. He keeps telling his students that the future _____ (belong) to the well-educated.

2. When I arrive at home, I smell something _____ (burn) in the kitchen.

3. I have a lot of readings _____ (complete) before the end of this term.

4. _____ (encourage) by the advances in technology, many farmers have set up wind farms on their land.

5. If he _____ (follow) my advice, he wouldn't have lost his job.

6. For breakfast he only drinks juice from fresh fruit _____ (grow) on his own farm.

7. His first book _____ (publish) next month is based on a true story.

8. Tom is looking for the watch his uncle _____ (give) him last month.

9. You'd better stay until the rain _____ (stop).

10. I _____ (ride) my bicycle to the bookshop when it suddenly began to rain. I was all wet through.

11. Richard turned off the computer after he had finished _____ (write) the email.

12. It is reported that more new teaching buildings _____ (build) in our school in the next semester.

13. Great changes have taken place since we _____ (enter) E-Times.

14. My mother isn't at home now. She _____ (ask) to go shopping.

15. Many buildings in the city need repairing, but the one _____ (repair) first is the library.

● 选词成句：选择合适的单词完成下列各句

1. The radio
    (A) tells
    (B) talks
    (C) says
    (D) speaks
    that there will be another heavy rain in Guangdong.

2. We are going to play basketball. Would you please
    (A) take
    (B) attend
    (C) join
    (D) take part in
    us?

3. He telephoned the travel agency to
    (A) order
    (B) arrange
    (C) take
    (D) book
    three air tickets to London.

4. Thousands of foreigners

(A) attended
(B) attained
(C) attracted
(D) attached

the Beijing Olympic Games.

5. The twins look almost alike, so I could not

(A) identify
(B) recognize
(C) distinguish
(D) classify

them.

6. The boy threw a stone into the lake which

(A) broke
(B) disturbed
(C) bothered
(D) interrupted

the smooth surface of

the water.

7. Your homework is well done. Just

(A) create
(B) connect
(C) correct
(D) control

some small mistakes in it.

8. I don't like this blouse because it doesn't

(A) fix
(B) accept
(C) compare
(D) match

my slack very well.

● 句子改错：判断句中画线动词的形式是否正确，错误的请在横线上改正，
没有错误请画√

1. The living room is clean and tidy, with a dining table already <u>laying</u> for a meal to be
cooked.

Correction _____ ;

2. He <u>played</u> basketball regularly for many years when he was young.

Correction _____ ;

3. I hear they've promoted Tom, but he didn't mention <u>having promoted</u> when we talked on the phone.

Correction _____ ;

4. <u>Reminding</u> not to miss the flight at 15:20, the manager set out for the airport in a hurry.

Correction _____ ;

5. I walked slowly through the market, where people <u>sell</u> all kinds of fruits and vegetables. I studied the prices carefully and bought what I needed.

Correction _____ ;

6. <u>Seeing</u> from the top of the tower, the south foot of the mountain is a sea of trees.

Correction _____ ;

7. Dina, <u>struggling</u> for months to find a job as a waitress, finally took a position at a local advertising agency.

Correction _____ ;

8. Lots of rescue workers were working around the clock, <u>sending</u> supplies to Yushu, Qinghai province after the earthquake.

Correction _____ ;

9. Tom will call me as soon as he <u>got</u> home.

Correction _____ ;

10. Lisa is busy packing her luggage because she <u>is leaving</u> for America for vacation.

Correction _____.

Answers & Explanations

Diagnostic Test

1. D 题目理解为"——昨天的展览怎么样？——非常吵，但是没有打扰到我。"考生可根据 but 推断 noisy 并没有影响到说话者。impress 表示"给……留下深刻印象"；hurt 表示"伤害"；change 表示"改变"。

2. B 题目考查考生对词组的把握：prefer to do...rather than do... 表示"宁愿做……而不愿做……"。题目理解为"比起出门，我宁愿待在家里"。

3. B 题目理解为"主题为'城市，让生活更美好'的 2010 年上海世博会吸引了来自世界各国的人们"。attend 表示"参加"；allow 表示"允许"；advise 表示"建议"。

4. A 题目考查考生区分两个词组的能力：used to do sth. 表示"过去常常做某事"，而 be used to doing sth. 表示"习惯做某事"。题目理解为"这个年轻人以前常常开车去上班，但是现在他习惯走路去上班"。

5. D 题目理解为"——看！那里有一棵高大的树，你能爬上去吗，戴夫？——是的，让我试一下。"have a try 表示"尝试一下"，考生可根据 let sb. do sth.（让某人做某事）确定第二个空，从而选出答案。fall off 表示"跌落"；send up 表示"上升"；come down 表示"下来"，三个词组都不符合题目句意。

6. A take sth. with sb. 表示"某人随身携带某物"，在时间状语从句中经常用一般现在时表示将来发生的事情。题目理解为"——外面下雨了，黛西，带把雨伞吧。——谢谢，下周来的时候就还给你"。

7. B 题目考查 have been to 和 have gone to 的用法。have been to 表示"曾去过但已回来"，have gone to 表示"曾去过但没有回来"。

8. C 题目考查动词的过去进行时态：be (was, were) + doing。题目理解为"我第一次遇到莉萨是在三年前，那时我们在同一家广播站工作"。were working 表示的是过去某段时间的持续工作状态。

9. B agree with 后加 sb.，表示"同意某人的意见"；agree on/in 后加 sth.，表示"与……保持一致"；it doesn't matter 表示"无所谓，没关系"。题目理解为"——恐怕没有人会赞同你。——我觉得无所谓。"

10. C 题目理解为"当你敲门的时候，我正在和我的父母看电视"。过去进行时表示"过去某一时间正在进行的动作"。

11. A 以 please 开头的句子通常是祈使句，祈使句用一般现在时和动词原形。will be 为一般将来时，表示"将要……"。

12. D 题目理解为"我哥哥当了十年的英语教师了"。It has been + 一段时间 + since... 表示"从……起已有多长时间了"。

13. D hand out 表示"分发"；put out 表示"熄灭；出版"；sell out 表示"售完"；give out 表示"分发；用尽"。题目理解为"这个姑娘将其全部存款捐给了西南地区遭受严重旱灾的人们"。

14. A give up 表示"放弃"；fix up 表示"修补"；cheer up 表示"振作起来"；put up 表示"举起；张贴"。题目理解为"你不应该放弃希望，一切都会好起来的"。

15. C 题目考查 there be 句型和"主将从现"，即主句用将来时，从句用一般现在时。

句子填空

1. belongs 时态为一般现在时。

2. burning smell 为感官动词，smell sth. doing 意为"闻到某物有……的味道"。

3. to complete 不定式作后置定语，修饰 readings。

4. Encouraged 主语为 many farmers，过去分词表被动。

5. had followed if 条件句的过去虚拟，主句用 would + 完成时，if 条件句用过去完成时。

6. grown grown 表示一种属性状态——已经长成的。

7. to be published 不定式作后置定语，修饰 book，book 需要"被出版"。

8. gave 由 last month 可知用过去式。

9. stops 时态为一般现在时。

10. was riding "突然开始下雨的时候，我正在骑自行车去书店"，用过去进行时。

11. writing finish + doing，意为"完成某事"。

12. will be built "下学期要建造"，用将来时，且 buildings 需要"被建造"。

13. entered "自从我们进入了 E 时代，发生了巨大变化"，since 后用过去时。

14. was asked 现在不在家，是之前被叫去购物了，因此用过去时的被动语态。

15. to be repaired 不定式作后置定语，修饰 one building，building 需要"被维修"。

选词成句

1. C tell 表示"告诉"；talk 表示"谈论"；say 表示"说"；speak 表示"讲某种语言"。

2. C 题目理解为"我们打算去打篮球，你要加入我们么？"attend 后面一般接 to；take part in 后面一般接 sth.。

3. D book 表示"预订"。

4. C attend to 表示"参加"。

5. C 题目理解为"这对双胞胎看起来很像,我无法区分他们"。identify 表示"鉴别,明确身份";
recognize 表示"认出";distinguish 表示"区分,鉴别";classify 表示"分类"。

6. B 题目理解为"小男孩将一块石头扔到湖里,打破了本来平静的水面"。break 表示"弄坏,弄碎";
disturb 表示"打破……的平静";bother 表示"烦扰,使恼怒";interrupt 表示"中断,打断"。

7. C correct 表示"改正"。

8. D 题目理解为"我不喜欢这件衬衫,因为它和我的裤子不是很搭"。

句子改错

1. laid 被动语态,表示 dining table "被布置好了"。

2. √

3. having been promoted mention + doing 表示"提及某事",已经"被升职"用被动形式 -ed +
完成时态:have been done。

4. Reminded "被提醒"用被动形式 -ed。

5. were selling 过去进行时表示一种状态,"人们正在卖各种各样的果蔬"。

6. Seen mountain 是"被看"的,因此用被动形式 seen。

7. having struggled "迪娜在找到当地广告公司的职位之前,做了几个月的服务员",表示"……
之前做的事情"应该用完成时 have + done,ing 形式表示主动。

8. √

9. gets as soon as 引导状语从句,"主将从现"。

10. √

Diagnostic Test

1. **I bought a shirt because it was good in quality and _____ in price.**

   A. reasonable

   B. valuable

   C. comfortable

   D. enjoyable

2. **According to the new research, gardening is a more _____ exercise for older women than jogging or swimming.**

   A. mental

   B. physical

   C. effective

   D. efficient

3. **The church is a _____ example of Gothic architecture.**

   A. profound

   B. realistic

   C. practical

   D. perfect

4. **Mr. Black is very happy because the clothes made in his factory have never been _____ than now.**

   A. popular

   B. more popular

   C. most popular

   D. the most popular

5. **It took _____ a day to complete the task. And I have stayed up for 2 days without sleep.**

   A. other than

B. more than

C. rather than

D. less than

6. It's high time you had your hair cut; it's getting _____.

    A. too much long

    B. much too long

    C. long too much

    D. too long much

7. If I find someone who looks like the suspect, my _____ reaction will be to tell the police.

    A. physical

    B. immediate

    C. sensitive

    D. sudden

8. Now the air in our city is _____ than it used to be. Something must be done to stop it.

    A. very good

    B. much better

    C. rather bad

    D. even worse

9. Don't believe the advertisement. This kind of camera is _____ it says.

    A. as good as

    B. not as good as

    C. as well as

    D. not as well as

10. Matthew came to Beijing in 2005. He has been here _____ than you.

    A. long

    B. longer

    C. longest

    D. the longest

11. Have you watched the TV program last night? It is so _____. Everyone enjoys a lot.

    A. boring

    B. funny

C. surprising

D. terrible

12. **No one is _____ Lucy in the class.**

    A. so tallest as

    B. as taller as

    C. so taller as

    D. as tall as

13. **The Yangtze River is one of _____ in the world.**

    A. the longest river

    B. longest rivers

    C. the longest rivers

    D. longer rivers

14. **The number of giant pandas is getting _____, because their living areas are becoming farmlands.**

    A. less and less

    B. larger and larger

    C. smaller and smaller

    D. fewer and fewer

15. **China is _____ country in the world.**

    A. the third largest

    B. the largest third

    C. the third large

    D. a third largest

Knowledge Points

1. 形容词比较级构成

考生需要多注意关于形容词的比较级及最高级的使用方法以及相关表达，因为这是 TOEFL®
Junior ™中常见的对于形容词的考查点。在平常的练习中，考生可多积累相关知识点。

类别	构成方法	原级	比较级	最高级
单音节和 少数双音节	+er，+est	long	longer	longest
	+r，+st	late	later	latest
	y-i+er，+est	easy	easier	easiest
	双写 +er，+est	big	bigger	biggest
多音节和 部分双音节	在原级前 +more，+most	beautiful	more beautiful	most beautiful

原级	比较级	最高级
good/well	better	best
many/much	more	most
bad/ill	worse	worst
little	less	least
far	farther 较远/further 进一步	farthest/furthest
old	older 年纪较大的/elder 较年长的	oldest/eldest

2. 形容词原级的用法

- 用 very/so/too/enough/quite 等表示绝对概念的副词修饰时用形容词原级
- 表示 A 和 B 某方面程度相同：A is + as + 形容词原级 + as + B
- 表示 A 和 B 某方面程度不同：A is not + as/so + 形容词原级 + as + B
- 表示 A 是 B 的几倍：A is + 倍数 + as + 形容词原级 + as + B
- 表示 A 是 B 的一半：A is half as + 形容词原级 + as + B

3. 形容词比较级的用法

- 表示 A 和 B 两者比较：A is + 比较级 + than + B，关键词为 than
- 用 a little，a bit，a few，a lot，much，even，still，far，rather，any 等表示程度的副词修饰形容词时，用比较级
- 表示 A 是 B 的几倍：A is + 倍数 + 比较级 + than B
- 表示越来越……：the + 比较级，the + 比较级

4. 形容词最高级的用法

- 表示三者或三者以上比较用最高级，最高级前通常加 the

- 表示 A 是最……的 B 之一：A is one of the + 最高级 + B
- 表示第几最……：序数词 + 最高级

5. -ing 形容词和 -ed 形容词的区别

-ing 形容词常表示"令人……的"，用来形容物；而 -ed 形容词常表示"感到……的"，用来形容人。例如：

The book is interesting.

He is interested in reading books.

6. 形容词词义辨析

TOEFL® Junior ™ 考题中会出现涉及形容词词义辨析的题目，即四个选项皆为形容词，但它们之间并无实际联系，从而使考生因为不清楚词义而混淆。

7. 以 -ly 结尾的形容词

考生要注意区分该类单词和副词的不同。例如 friendly，lovely，daily 等等。

8. 形容词的排列顺序

当名词有两个或以上的形容词修饰时，这些形容词的词序通常遵循一定的规则。词序依次为：

- 限定词 (the，that，a...)
- 描绘性的词 (beautiful，interesting...)
- 表示大小、长短、高低等的词 (tall，high，small...)
- 表示年龄、新旧的词 (new，young，old...)
- 表示颜色的词 (red，pink，grey...)
- 表示国籍、出处的词 (Chinese，English，rural...)
- 表示材料的词 (wooden，silky，plastic...)

9. "定冠词 + 形容词"表示一类人

常见词有 good/bad，rich/poor，young/old，deaf/blind，black/white，living/dead 等等。例如 the young 表示"年轻人"。

Assignment & Exercise

● 句子填空：选用括号里的词的正确形式完成句子

1. He is _____ (bad) at learning math. He is much _____ (bad) at Chinese and he is the _____ (bad) at English.

2. He is one of the _____ (friendly) people in the class, I think.

3. An orange is a little _____ (big) than an apple, but much _____ (small) than a watermelon.

4. This book is not as _____ (interesting) as that one.

5. Most of the students think the lion is much _____ (dangerous) than the bear and the lion is the _____ (dangerous) animal in the world.

6. Nowadays English is _____ (important) than any other subject.

7. Things are getting _____ and _____ (bad).

8. There are _____ (few) boys than girls in our class.

9. Sue is a little _____ (beautiful) than her sister.

10. He comes to school much _____ (early) than I.

11. Your classroom is _____ (wide) and _____ (bright) than ours.

12. I'm _____, but she is _____ than me (beautiful).

13. Today is the _____ (busy) day I have ever had.

14. I think pizza is the _____ (delicious) food of all.

15. The higher you climb, the _____ (cold) it will be.

● **翻译：根据汉语提示完成句子，注意形容词的使用**

1. 这部电影太无聊了。

   _____

2. 这主意听起来不错。

   _____

3. 这本书不如那本书有意义。

   _____

4. 她是我们中间最漂亮的。

   _____

5. 我是全班学习最好的。

   _____

6. 我有些有趣的事情想要告诉你。

   _____

7. 今天报纸上没有什么重要的内容。

   _____

8. 我的房间至少比你的房间大 3 倍。

   _____

● **选词成句：选择合适的单词完成下列各句**

1. Birds can fly _____; eagles can fly _____ than birds. They fly _____ in the world. (high, higher, the highest)

2. Which can swim _____, fish or sharks? (well, better, best)

3. The green book is a _____ book, but the red one is much _____ than the green one. It's the _____ book in the bookshop. (nice, nicer, nicest)

4. I think that book is _____ for you. (good, better)

5. Look, Janet is jumping _____ than Mike. (high, higher)

6. We were all _____ at this _____ news. (surprised, surprising)

7. The U.S.A. is one of _____ countries in the world. (richer, most rich, the richest)

8. Mr. Hare runs much _____ than Mr. Turtle. Mr. Hare needn't run _____ now. (fast, faster)

9. In the gym, Tommy is playing table tennis _____ than Jimmy. (well, better)

10. The film is the _____ film of all. (horrible, more horrible, most horrible)

11. It's summer now. The weather is getting _____. (hot and hot, hotter and hotter, hottest and hottest)

12. This radio is not so _____ as that one. (cheap, cheaper, cheapest)

Answers & Explanations

Diagnostic Test

1. A 题目理解为"我买了一件衬衫,因为它质量好且价钱合理"。reasonable 表示"合理的"; valuable 表示"有价值的"; comfortable 表示"舒服的"; enjoyable 表示"有趣的"。

2. C 题目理解为"根据新的研究,从事园艺工作对于大龄女性来说是比慢跑或游泳更为有效的锻炼"。mental 表示"心理的"; physical 表示"身体的"; effective 表示"有效的"; efficient 表示"效率高的"。

3. D 题目理解为"这间教堂是哥特式建筑的完美典范"。profound 表示"深奥的"; realistic 表示"实际的"; practical 表示"实用的"; perfect 表示"完美的"。

4. B 题目理解为"布莱克先生非常高兴，因为他的工厂生产的衣服从未比现在更受欢迎"。题目中出现 than，用形容词比较级形式。

5. B 题目理解为"完成这个任务花了一天多的时间，我已经两天没有睡觉了"。more than 表示"多于……"。

6. B 题目理解为"你该去剪头发了，它长得太长了"。表示"太长"用 much too long。

7. B 题目理解为"如果我发现谁长得像嫌疑犯，我的直接反应就是告诉警察"。physical 表示"身体的"；immediate 表示"立即的，直接的"；sensitive 表示"敏感的"；sudden 表示"突然的，意外的"。

8. D 题目理解为"现在我们城市的空气比以前要差很多，我们应该做点什么来阻止这种状况"。题目中出现 than 要用形容词比较级形式。

9. B 题目理解为"不要相信这个广告，这款相机不如广告说得那么好"。good 是形容词，as good as 表示"和……一样好"。

10. B 出现 than 要用形容词比较级形式。

11. B 题目理解为"你看了昨晚的电视节目吗？太有趣了，大家都很喜欢"。boring 表示"无聊的"；funny 表示"有趣的"；surprising 表示"惊人的"；terrible 表示"糟糕的"。

12. D as tall as 表示"和……一样高"。

13. C 题目理解为"长江是世界上最长的河流之一"，用 one of + the + 形容词最高级 + 名词复数。

14. A 题目理解为"大熊猫的数量越来越少了，因为它们的居住区域变成了耕地"。用形容词比较级 + 形容词比较级表示"越来越……"，number 表示数量时不可数，比较级要用 less 而不是 fewer。

15. A 题目理解为"中国是世界第三大国"，用 the + 序数词 + 形容词最高级 + 名词。

句子填空

1. bad; worse; worst

2. most friendly

3. bigger; smaller

4. interesting

5. more dangerous; most dangerous

6. more important

7. worse; worse

8. fewer

9. more beautiful

10. earlier

11. wider; brighter

12.	beautiful; more beautiful

13.	busiest

14.	most delicious

15.	colder

翻译

1.	The movie is rather/too boring.

2.	This idea sounds great.

3.	This book is not as meaningful as that one.

4.	She is the most beautiful girl among us.

5.	I study the best in my class.

6.	I have something interesting to tell you.

7.	There is nothing significant in today's newspaper.

8.	My room is at least three times bigger than yours.

选词成句

1.	high; higher; the highest

2.	better

3.	nice; nicer; nicest

4.	good

5.	higher

6.	surprised; surprising

7.	the richest

8.	faster; fast

9.	better

10.	most horrible

11.	hotter and hotter

12.	cheap

Chapter 03

Adverb
（副词）

Diagnostic Test

1. The committee is discussing the problem right now. It will _____ have been solved by the end of next week.

   A. eagerly

   B. hopefully

   C. immediately

   D. gradually

2. Father _____ goes to the gym with us although he dislikes going there.

   A. hardly

   B. seldom

   C. sometimes

   D. nothing

3. The accident is _____ fresh in my memory than when it happened.

   A. little

   B. more

   C. no less

   D. without

4. I am not blaming anyone; I _____ say errors like this could be avoided.

   A. merely

   B. mostly

   C. rarely

   D. nearly

5. It was a nice house, but _____ too small for a family of five.

   A. rarely

   B. fairly

C. rather

D. pretty

6. **After two years' research, we now have a _____ better understanding of the disease.**

   A. very

   B. far

   C. fairly

   D. quite

7. **The horse is getting old and cannot run _____ it did.**

   A. as faster as

   B. so fast than

   C. so faster as

   D. as fast as

8. **The students are _____ young children between the ages of eleven and fourteen.**

   A. most

   B. almost

   C. mostly

   D. at most

9. **— Can I help you?**

   — Well, I'm afraid the box is _____ heavy for you to carry, but thank you all the same.

   A. so

   B. much

   C. very

   D. too

10. **— Excuse me, is this Ms. Jones's office?**

    — I'm sorry, but Ms. Jones _____ works here. She left about three weeks ago.

    A. not now

    B. no more

    C. not still

    D. no longer

11. **After the new technique was introduced, the factory produced _____ tractors in 1988 as the year before.**

    A. as twice many

B. as many twice

C. twice as many

D. twice many as

12. **How _____ can you finish the drawing?**

A. long

B. often

C. soon

D. rapid

13. **We all write _____, even when there's not much to say.**

A. now and then

B. by and by

C. step by step

D. more or less

14. **— Do you remember _____ he came?**

— Yes, I do. He came by car.

A. how

B. when

C. that

D. if

15. **A _____ road goes _____ from our college to the center.**

A. straight; straight

B. straightly; straightly

C. straight; straightly

D. straightly; straight

Knowledge Points

1. 副词的种类

种类	示例
时间和频率副词	now, then, today, tomorrow, yesterday, before, ago, soon, immediately, lately, early, sometimes, often, always, usually, already, yet, ever, never, seldom...

种类	示例
地点副词	outside, inside, upstairs, here, there, near, away, in, back, off, up, anywhere, somewhere, above, below, down, forward, back, across, along, around...
方式副词	quickly, happily, loudly, suddenly, luckily, badly, easily, fast, again...
程度副词	very, quite, rather, too, much, so, rather, almost...
疑问副词	how, when, where, why, how long, how far, how soon, how often...

2. 副词可作状语、表语

e.g. You speak English very well. 你英语讲得相当好。（作状语）

    I am here. 我在这里。（作表语）

3. 副词的位置

- 时间副词、地点副词和方式副词一般放在句子末尾。
- 频率副词可放在实义动词的前面，情态动词和助动词的后面。
- 疑问副词以及修饰整个句子的副词，通常放在句子或从句的前面。
- 否定副词位于句首，句子要倒装。

4. 副词的比较级和最高级

以 -ly 结尾的副词（除 early 外）须用 more 和 most。副词的比较级和最高级用法同形容词的比较级和最高级的用法基本一样。在含有最高级形式的句子中，the 有时可以省略。

5. 特殊表达法

- hard 表示"努力地，辛苦地；剧烈地，猛烈地"。

  hardly 表示"几乎不"。
- much too 表示"非常，极其，太"。

  too much 表示"太多"。

- close 表示"近"。

  closely 表示"仔细地"。

- late 表示"晚"。

  lately 表示"最近"。

- deep 表示"深"，多指空间上的深度。

  deeply 表示"深深地"，多指情感上的深度。

- high 表示"高"，多指空间上的高度。

  highly 表示程度，相当于 much。

- wide 表示"宽"，多指空间上的宽度。

  widely 表示"广泛地，在许多地方"。

- free 表示"免费的"。

  freely 表示"无限制地"。

- as such 表示上文提及的事或人。

  as much 表示"与……同量"。

  as many 表示"与……一样多"。

- how long 表示"多久，多长时间"，常用"for + 一段时间"和"since + 时间点"回答。

  how soon 表示"多快，多久以后"，常用"in + 时间段"回答。

  how often 表示"多长时间一次"，常用 once，twice，...times a week/month/year 等方式回答。

  how far 表示"多远"，用于对距离的提问。

- too，as well，also 用于肯定句。too，as well 多用于口语，一般位于句末；also 一般位于句中与动词连用。

- already 表示某事已经发生，主要用于肯定句；yet 表示期待某事发生，主要用于否定句和疑问句；still 表示某事还在进行，主要用于肯定句和疑问句，有时也可用于否定句。

- 比较级前可用 a little，a bit，slightly，a great deal，a lot，many，much 等词语表示不定量；用 far，completely，still 等词语表示程度或更进一步。

Assignment & Exercise

- **翻译：根据汉语提示完成句子，注意副词的使用**

1. 我几乎看不到报纸上的字。

    _____

2. 这道数学题太难了。

    _____

3. 我也不喜欢那个淘气的男孩。

    _____

4. 这个芯片这么小，以至于我都看不见它。

    _____

5. 我还没完成这项任务。

    _____

6. 仅仅让两个人在短时间内完成这么多的工作是不可能的。

    _____

7. 我跑得不够快，所以我根本追不上他们。

    _____

8. 你多久去一次那家餐厅呢?

    _____

● 选词成句：选择合适的单词完成下列各句

1. We decided not to climb the mountains because it was raining

    | (A) badly. |
    | (B) hardly. |
    | (C) strongly. |
    | (D) heavily. |

2.

(A) Unfortunately,
(B) Fortunately,
(C) Being fortunate,
(D) Being unfortunate,

I found that I forgot to take my purse with me when I

decided to pay the bills.

3. If we work with a strong will, we can overcome any difficulty,

(A) what
(B) how
(C) however
(D) whatever

great it is.

4. I walked eight miles today. I never guessed that I could walk

(A) much
(B) that
(C) such
(D) as

far.

5. We've

(A) already
(B) yet
(C) still
(D) also

watched that film.

6. He has to work

(A) lone
(B) lonely
(C) alone
(D) lonesome

at the office because everyone in his team has

finished their own work except him.

7. Oh, God! I must have gained too much weight. I can

(A) nearly
(B) hardly
(C) fairly
(D) quickly

put on my trousers.

8. The two friends were
(A) too
(B) so
(C) quite
(D) much
pleased to see each other that they talking on and

on in the park.

Answers & Explanations

Diagnostic Test

1. B 题目理解为"委员会正在讨论这个问题。它有希望在下周末得到解决"。eagerly 表示"急切地"；hopefully 表示"抱着希望地"；immediately 表示"立即地"；gradually 表示"逐渐地"。

2. C 题目理解为"父亲有时和我们一起去体育馆，即使他并不喜欢去那里"。hardly 表示"几乎不"；seldom 表示"很少"；sometimes 表示"有时"；nothing 表示"没有东西"。用 hardly 或 seldom 都不符合句子的逻辑。

3. C 题目理解为"我对这场事故记忆犹新"。no less than 表示"不少于，多于"，也就是"这场事故在我记忆中跟发生的时候是一样新的"。

4. A 题目理解为"我不是在批评某个人，我只是说像这样的错误是可以被避免的"。merely 表示"仅仅是"；mostly 表示"主要地"；rarely 表示"很少"；nearly 表示"几乎，差不多"。

5. C 题目理解为"这是一间好房子，但是对于一家五口来说太小了"。rarely 表示"很少"；fairly 和 pretty 都表示褒义，为程度副词，译为"相当地"，不能和 too 连用；rather 同样表示"相当地"，含有贬义色彩，可以和 too 连用。

6. B 题目理解为"经过两年的研究，我们现在对这种疾病有了更为深刻的了解"，在 very, far, fairly 和 quite 中，只有 far 可以用来修饰比较级。

7. D 同级比较的结构为：as + 副词原形 + as。

8. C 题目理解为"学生主要是年龄在 11 岁到 14 岁之间的孩子"。most 表示"多数的"；almost 表示"几乎，差不多"；mostly 表示"主要地，大部分地"；at most 表示"至多"。

9. D 固定表达 too...for sb. to do，表示"对于某人来说太……而不能……"，意思是"对于你来说，这个盒子太重了，你拿不动"。

10. D 题目理解为"——打扰了，请问这是琼斯女士的办公室么？——很抱歉，琼斯女士不在这里工作了，她在三个星期前就离开了。"no longer 表示时间不再延续，意思是"如今不再"；no more 着重表示数量或程度的减少，意思是"再也没有更多（大）的数量（程度）"，no more 等于 not...any more。

11. C 固定用法，表示倍数的词或其他程度副词作修饰语应放在 as...as 结构的前面。

12. C 题目理解为"你多久能完成这幅画？"long 指一段时间，不能与 finish 连用；often 指时间频度，即每隔一段时间发生一次动作；rapid 是形容词，不能修饰动词。

13. A 题目理解为"我们会不时地写信，即使有时候没有多少话要说"。now and then 表示"时而，不时地"；by and by 表示"不久"；step by step 表示"逐步地"；more or less 表示"或多或少"。

14. A by car 表示"开车"，是一种方式，对于方式的提问要用 how。

15. A straight 兼具形容词与副词词性。

翻译

1. I can hardly see the words on newspaper.

2. This math question is much/rather too difficult.

3. I don't like that naughty boy either.

4. This chip is too small for me to see it easily.

5. I haven't finished this task yet.

6. It is impossible for merely two people to accomplish so much work in a short period.

7. I cannot run fast enough to catch up with them.

8. How often have you been to that restaurant?

选词成句

1. D 形容"雨下得很大"用 heavily。badly 表示"恶劣地，严重地"；hardly 表示"几乎不"；strongly 表示"强有力地"。

2. A 结账时发现没带钱包是件很不幸的事情，排除选项 B 和 C。副词可放在句首，作整句话的状语。

3. C however = no matter how，题目理解为"如果我们在工作中有强烈的意志，就可以克服任何困难，无论困难有多么大"。

4. B that = so，that far 特指"eight miles"。

5. A already 表示某事已经发生，用于完成时态的肯定句中。

6. C alone 为副词，表示"独自地"，修饰 work，其余三个选项均为形容词。

7. B 通过前一句"我一定是胖了很多"，可以推断后一句应该是"我穿不上我的裤子了"。hardly 表示"几乎不"。

8. B 整句话理解为"这两个朋友如此高兴见到对方，以至于他们一直在公园里聊天。"so...that... 表示"如此……以至于……"。

Chapter 04

Noun
（名词）

Diagnostic Test

1. **Jim sold most of his things. He has hardly _____ left in the house.**

   A. anything

   B. everything

   C. nothing

   D. something

2. **I bought a dress for only 10 dollars in a sale; it was a real _____.**

   A. exchange

   B. bargain

   C. trade

   D. business

3. **The top leaders of the two countries are holding talks in a friendly _____.**

   A. atmosphere

   B. state

   C. situation

   D. phenomenon

4. **— Has she had much _____ in teaching English?**

   — No. She is just a new hand.

   A. base

   B. future

   C. energy

   D. experience

5. **The football team of No. 1 Middle School invited us to a match and we decided to accept the _____.**

   A. chance

B. challenge

C. match

D. game

6. **In dealing with public relations, we should make every _____ to prevent the conflict in personality.**

   A. effect

   B. power

   C. energy

   D. effort

7. **The _____ on his face told me that he was angry.**

   A. impression

   B. sight

   C. appearance

   D. expression

8. **Many graduates in China do their best to go abroad to seek their _____.**

   A. luck

   B. chance

   C. fortune

   D. fate

9. **We have worked out the plan and now we must put it into _____.**

   A. fact

   B. reality

   C. practice

   D. deed

10. **We volunteered to collect money to help the _____ of the earthquake.**

    A. victims

    B. folks

    C. fellows

    D. villagers

11. **— Would you like some _____?**

    — Thank you. I'm not thirsty.

    A. sandwiches

B. mooncakes

C. bread

D. orange

12. — Where is Tom?

— He's left _____ saying that he has something important to do.

A. an excuse

B. a sentence

C. news

D. a message

13. _____ is nice and clean.

A. The air today

B. The today air

C. The airs

D. The air of today

14. There is a good _____ for you. I've found your lost watch.

A. news

B. ideas

C. messages

D. thoughts

15. There are about 50 _____ in our school.

A. woman doctors

B. women teachers

C. woman teachers

D. woman workers

Knowledge Points

1. 在 TOEFL® Junior ™ 考试中，对名词的主要考查点是其意思。考生对名词类选择题不必过于担忧，因为此类考题难度比较低。平时可多注意总结并积累一些名词，弄清楚意思即可。

2. 名词分为可数名词和不可数名词，考生必须掌握名词的单复数形式，这对英语学习者是最基础的要求。可数名词复数构成的规则有：

- 一般情况下，单词后面 + s

- 以 -s, -x, -ch, -sh 结尾的单词后面 + es

- 以辅音字母加 -y 结尾的单词，把 y 变为 i，后面 + es

- 以元音字母加 -y 结尾的单词后面 + s

- 以 f(fe) 结尾的单词，把 f(fe) 变为 ves，例如：wolf-wolves；个别可直接 + s，例如：roof-roofs

- 以 ce, se, ze, (d)ge 等结尾的单词，后面 + s

- 以 -o 结尾的单词，有些 + es，例如：heroes，potatoes 等；有些 + s，例如：radios，zoos 等

- 个别单词变复数只需改变名词中的元音字母，例如：man-men，tooth-teeth 等

- 有些名词的单复数形式相同，读音也相同，例如：Chinese，sheep 等

- 个别单词的变法不规则，例如：mouse-mice 等

3. 不可数名词需要计量时，可用 "数词 / 冠词 + 量词 + of + 不可数名词"，例如：a piece of paper，two cups of tea 等。

4. 有些名词既可以是可数名词，也可以是不可数名词，例如：room（空间）/a room（一个房间）。

Assignment & Exercise

- 翻译：根据英文提示完整翻译句子

1. He is a friend of my elder brother's.

   _____

2. The girl was washing greens.

   _____

3. Please hand in your papers at once.

   _____

4. Aunt Mary lost her good looks when she was old.

   _____

5. He was in the blues because of the cold weather.

   _____

6. She always takes pains with her work.

   _____

7. They choose the boy monitor.

   _____

8. There are the works of Shakespeare in the library.

   _____

9. They got much information from those new books.

   _____

10. I want to have a word with you about the problem.

    _____

● 选词成句一：选择合适的单词完成下列各句

1. I recognize her _____ at once. (voice/sound/noise)

2. They lived in a small _____. (home/house/family)

3. Lucy wants to be a singer. She thinks it's an interesting _____. (work/job)

4. He asks me many _____; I can just answer some of them. (problems/questions)

5. My parents always let me have my own _____ of living. (way/method)

6. Many countries are increasing their use of natural gas, wind and other forms of _____. (energy/source/power)

7. What's your favorite _____, swimming or running? (sport/game)

8. He is a good _____. (cook/cooker)

9. Please remember to give the horse some tree _____. (leafs/leaves)

10. He gives me some _____. (advice/advices)

● 选词成句二：选择合适的单词完成下列各句

1. All children should learn _____. (manner/manners)

2. The prisoner was put in _____. (iron/irons)

3. The bridge is built of _____ and steel. (iron/irons)

4. The cavalry joined _____ with the police to stamp out the riot. (force/forces)

5. His brother served in the Air _____ during the war. (Force/Forces)

6. Herbert inherited a large _____ from his father. (property/properties)

7. The students are making an experiment to test the _____ of oxygen. (property/properties)

8. The balloon rose into the _____. (air/airs)

9. Joan used to put on _____ when there were young men around. (air/airs)

10. They are studying the _____ of Hemingway. (work/works)

Answers & Explanations

Diagnostic Test

1. A 题目理解为"吉姆卖掉了大部分东西,房子里几乎没剩下什么"。前面有 hardly,所以不能选 nothing。anything 常用于否定句中。

2. B 题目理解为"在大减价中,我只花了 10 美元就买到了一条连衣裙,真是太便宜了"。exchange 表示"交换;兑换";bargain 表示"便宜货;交易";trade 表示"贸易;商业";business 表示"商业;生意"。

3. A 题目理解为"两国最高领导人在友好的气氛中进行会谈"。atmosphere 表示"气氛";state 表示"状态";situation 表示"状况;形势";phenomenon 表示"现象"。

4. D 题目理解为"——她有很多教授英语的经验吗? ——不,她还只是一个新手。"base 表示"基础";future 表示"未来";energy 表示"能量";experience 表示"经验"。

5. B 题目理解为"第一中学的足球队邀请我们参加一场比赛,我们决定接受这个挑战"。chance 表示"机会";challenge 表示"挑战";match 表示"比赛";game 表示"比赛"。

6. D 题目理解为"在处理公共关系时,我们应该努力防止性格上的'冲突'"。make every effort 表示"努力做……";effect 表示"影响";power 表示"能力;权力";energy 表示"精力;能量"。

7. D 题目理解为"他脸上的表情告诉我,他很生气"。impression 表示"印象;感觉";sight 表示"视力;眼界";appearance 表示"外貌;外表";expression 表示"表情;表达"。

8. C 题目理解为"许多中国的毕业生全力以赴去国外寻找发展的机会"。seek one's fortune 为固定表达,表示"寻找出路,寻找发迹的机会";luck 表示"运气";chance 表示"机会";fate 表示"命运"。

9. C 题目理解为"我们已经制订出计划了,现在就必须把它付诸实践"。put into practice 为固定搭配,表示"实行,实施";fact 表示"事实,真相";reality 表示"现实;实际";deed 表示"行为"。

10. A 题目理解为"为帮助地震中的灾民,我们自愿筹款"。victim 表示"受害者;灾民";folk 表示"人们;亲属;家属";fellow 表示"家伙;同伴";villager 表示"村民"。

11. D 通过"I'm not thirsty."推断上文问的应该是要不要饮料。sandwich 表示"三明治";mooncake 表示"月饼";bread 表示"面包";orange 表示"橙汁"。

12. D 题目理解为"——Tom 在哪里? ——他留话说有些重要的事情要做。"excuse 表示"借口,理由;辩解";sentence 表示"句子;判决";news 表示"新闻;消息";message 表示"便条;信息,消息"。

13. A 题目理解为"今天的空气很好很清新"。选项 B 中 today 没有用所有格，排除。选项 C 中 air 不可数，排除。选项 D 中 today 前不能加介词，排除。

14. A 题目理解为"有个好消息告诉你，我找到了你丢的手表"。news 表示"新闻；消息"；idea 表示"想法；主意"；message 表示"便条；信息，消息"；thought 表示"想法；思想"。

15. B 题目理解为"我们学校大概有 50 名女老师"。woman 修饰名词复数时，本身也要变成复数形式。

翻译

1. 他是我哥哥的一个朋友。

2. 这个女孩正在洗菜。

3. 请立刻把你们的试卷交上来。

4. 年老的玛丽阿姨失去了花容月貌。（年老色衰）

5. 因为天气寒冷，他心情忧郁。

6. 她一向工作很努力。

7. 他们选这个男孩当班长。

8. 图书馆里有些莎士比亚的著作。

9. 他们从那些新书中得到了很多信息。

10. 我想和你讨论一下这个问题。

选词成句一

1. voice sound 多用来表示大自然的声音，noise 多表示噪音。

2. house house 表示住所。

3. job work 多指生产或完成某项工作所需的体力的或脑力的努力或活动，为不可数名词。job 多指为换取报酬而进行的日常活动，尤指作为某人的手艺、行业或职业的工作，为可数名词。

4. questions question 经常与 answer 搭配，problem 则常与 solution 搭配。

5. way way of living 表示"生活方式"。

6. energy energy 表示"能源；能量"。

7. sport sport 表示"体育运动"。

8. cook cook 表示"厨师"，cooker 表示"炊具"。

9. leaves leaf 的复数形式为 leaves。

10. advice advice 为不可数名词。

选词成句二

1. manners manners 表示"礼貌；规矩；习俗"。

2. irons irons 表示"镣铐"。

3. iron iron 表示"铁"。

4. forces join forces with sb. 表示"与某人联合（会师）"。

5. Force Air Force 表示"空军"。

6. property property 表示"财产"。

7. properties properties 表示"性能"。

8. air air 表示"天空"。

9. airs put on airs 表示"摆架子"。

10. works works 表示"著作"。

Chapter 05

Preposition
(介词)

Diagnostic Test

1. If you really have to leave during the meeting, you'd better leave _____ the back door.
   A. for
   B. by
   C. across
   D. out

2. There were a lot of people standing at the door and the small girl couldn't get _____.
   A. between
   B. through
   C. across
   D. beyond

3. When asked about their preference about the movies, many young people are _____ sci-fi movies.
   A. in terms of
   B. in need of
   C. in favor of
   D. in praise of

4. Would you look _____ the paper for me and see if there are any obvious mistakes?
   A. around
   B. into
   C. up
   D. through

5. Everybody was touched _____ words after they heard her moving story.
   A. beyond
   B. without

C. of

D. in

6. **Thousands of people turned _____ to watch yesterday's football match.**

A. on

B. in

C. around

D. out

7. **I tried phoning her office, but I couldn't get _____.**

A. along

B. on

C. to

D. through

8. **A great man shows his greatness _____ the way he treats little men.**

A. under

B. with

C. on

D. by

9. **Again and again the doctor looked _____ the crying girl, but he couldn't find out what was wrong with her.**

A. over

B. after

C. for

D. out

10. **— The light in the office is still on.**

— Oh, I forget to turn it _____.

A. off

B. on

C. up

D. down

11. **It's getting warmer and warmer. The flowers start to come _____.**

A. in

B. over

C. out

D. on

12. **The plane takes _____ from Beijing Capital Airport and lands in London.**

A. up

B. out

C. away

D. off

13. **Tina and Mary are talking _____ the phone _____ their school rules.**

A. on; about

B. to; about

C. in; about

D. on; with

14. **Everyone of us is looking forward _____ getting a good result.**

A. on

B. in

C. to

D. at

15. **I got an e-mail this morning. It was _____ my foreign friend, Tony.**

A. in

B. on

C. at

D. from

Knowledge Points

1. 在 TOEFL® Junior ™考试中，考查介词使用的题目多侧重于动词与介词的搭配。同一个动词搭配不同的介词含义不同，考生需加以区别。此外，考生要熟悉常用的介词及其使用方法及含义。

2. 介词是一种虚词，用来表示它后面的名词或代词同句中其他某个成分之间的关系。介词在句中不能单独使用，必须连同它的宾语（即后面的名词或代词）构成介词词组后，才能作句子成分。常用介词有：

● 表示时间

at 多用于表示具体的钟点时刻，例如 at six。

in 表示一段时间，泛指年、月、四季或某一天，例如 in winter, in the morning。

on 主要用于描述具体时间、星期或具体某一天，例如 on Wednesday, on April 1st。

for 后常接时间段，一般动词用完成时态。

from 表示开始的时间，例如 from now on。

before/after 表示"在……之前"或"在……之后"。

until/till 表示"直到某时"，固定搭配有 not...until...

during 后加时间段，表示"在……期间"。

by 后加时间点，表示"到……以前为止"，多用于完成时态。

● 表示地点方位

in/on/to/at

over/above

in front of/in the front of

below/under

3. 介词用法

● between & among

between 常表示"在……（两者）之间"，between 可以和 and 连用。

among 常表示"在……（三者或三者以上的人或物）之间"。

● across & through & over & past

across 一般表示"从……表面穿过"，例如"过河"用 across the river。

through 一般表示"从……中间穿过"，例如"透过窗户往外"用 through the window。

over 表示"在空间范围之上越过、超过"，例如"飞过一座山"用 fly over a mountain。

past 表示"经过"，例如"路过一幢房子"可用 walk past a house。

● for & to & towards

for 常用在 leave, start 之后，表示运动方向或目的。

to 常用在 go, come, return, move 等词之后，表示目的地。

towards 只表示运动的方向。

● after & behind

after 意为"在……之后"，可表示时间、位置等。

behind 意为"在……之后"，只表示空间位置。

- in & with & by

  三个词都可以表示"用"。

  in 主要表示"用语言、声音、原材料等"。

  with 表示"用具体有形的实物"。

  by 表示"用……手段或方式",常跟动名词。

- but & except & besides

  三个词都可以表示"除……之外"。

  but 常与含否定意义的词连用。

  except 指从整体中排除(不再有)的意思,前面常有 all,every,any,no 及其他复合词。

  besides 指在原来的基础上加上(还有)的意思,前面常有 other,another,any other,a few 等词。

Assignment & Exercise

- 选词填空:选择合适的介词填入下列空格当中,可重复使用

  | with for of to through at in but around among |
  | until behind by like from without about on |

1. Last Sunday I was busy _____ my preparation of the final test.

2. My teacher was very angry _____ me because I was late _____ school three times this week.

3. This room is full _____ students and that one is filled _____ teachers.

4. I will invite some friends _____ my sixteenth birthday party.

5. The sunlight is coming in _____ the window.

6. My sister arrived _____ the airport _____ the morning of May 29.

7. It is well-known that the Earth moves _____ the Sun.

8. There is nothing _____ a card in the box.

9. I won't be back _____ September.

10. _____ the age _____ eighteen, he had written four books.

11. If you can't pass the exam, you'll fall _____ others.

12. China lies _____ the East of Asia and _____ the North of Australia.

13. You must stand _____ line when you are waiting _____ a bus.

14. It's very nice _____ you to get me two tickets _____ the World Cup.

15. The singer was given some presents _____ his fans.

16. Look, the birds are singing _____ the tree.

17. Please leave the classroom _____ all the windows closed.

18. My brother is ill today. He doesn't feel _____ eating anything.

19. It's too dangerous. You must keep the children away _____ the fire.

20. It's bad _____ you to go to work _____ breakfast.

21. You should apologize _____ her _____ stepping on her foot.

22. The students are sitting _____ the table, having their meals.

23. She is dressed _____ a blue skirt _____ white flowers.

24. We are doing better _____ English _____ our teacher's help.

25. Don't worry _____ me. Everything is going well _____ me.

26. There is going to be a report _____ American history _____ our school tomorrow.

27. Hip-hop is becoming more and more popular _____ teenagers.

28. I like clothes made _____ cotton.

29. You look tired. Instead _____ working indoors you should be out _____ a walk.

30. _____ my surprise, the Englishman gave up halfway _____ the end.

Answers & Explanations

Diagnostic Test

1. B 题目理解为"如果你不得不在会议期间离开，最好从后门出去"。by 表示一种方式。

2. B 题目理解为"门口站着很多人，这个小女孩无法穿过去"。get through 表示从立体的东西中间穿过去；get across 表示从东西表面穿过去。

3. C 题目理解为"当被问及对电影的喜好时，许多年轻人表示喜欢科幻电影"。in terms of 表示"就……而言"；in need of 表示"需要"；in favor of 表示"喜欢"；in praise of 表示"表扬"。

4. D 题目理解为"你能帮我检查一下这篇论文，看看里面是否有明显的错误吗？"look around 表示"环视，东张西望"；look into 表示"调查；观察"；look up 表示"查字典；仰视"；look through 表示"浏览；核查"。

5. A 题目理解为"在听了她感人的故事后，大家都被感动得一塌糊涂"。beyond words 表示"难以言表，无法用语言形容"。

6. A 题目理解为"成千上万的人打开电视机观看昨天的足球比赛"。turned on 表示"打开；接通"；turned in 表示"交还，上交"；turned around 表示"转身，转向"；turn out 表示"结果是；关掉"。

7. D 题目理解为"我试图打她办公室电话，但是不通"。get along 表示"前进；相处"；get on 表示"上车；进展"；get to 表示"到达"；get through 表示"通过；打通电话"。

8. D 题目理解为"这位伟人通过自己对待小人物的方式（可能很和蔼或者平易近人）显示了自己的伟大之处"。by the way 除了有"顺便说一句"的意思，还有"通过……的方式"的意思。

9. A 题目理解为"医生反复检查了这个一直哭的小女孩，但是找不出原因"。look over 表示"检查"；look after 表示"照顾"；look for 表示"寻找"；look out 表示"小心"。

10. A 题目理解为"——办公室的灯还亮着。——哦，我忘记关掉它了。"turn off 表示"关掉"；turn on 表示"接通；打开"；turn up 表示"开大，调大"；turn down 表示"关小，调低"。

11. C 题目理解为"天气越来越热，花都开始绽放了"。come out 表示"开花；出现"；come in 表示"进来"；come over 表示"顺便来访"；come on 表示"加油，快点；上演"。

12. D 题目理解为"飞机从北京首都机场起飞，在伦敦降落"。take off 表示"起飞"；take up 表示"占据"；take out 表示"拿出"；take away 表示"带走"。

13. A 题目理解为"Tina 和 Mary 正通过电话谈论学校的规则"。talk on the phone 表示"通过电话交谈"，talk about 表示"谈论……"。

14. C 题目理解为"我们中的每个人都希望得到一个好结果"。look forward to 为固定搭配，后接动词 ing 形式，表示"盼望，渴望"。

15. D 题目理解为"今天早上我收到了来自我的外国朋友 Tony 的电子邮件"。from 表示"来自……"。

选词成句

1.	with	16.	in
2.	with; for	17.	with
3.	of; with	18.	like
4.	to	19.	from
5.	through	20.	for; without
6.	at; on	21.	to; for
7.	around	22.	at
8.	but	23.	in; with
9.	until	24.	in; with
10.	At; of	25.	about; with
11.	behind	26.	on; in
12.	in; to	27.	among
13.	in; for	28.	from
14.	of; for	29.	of; for
15.	by	30.	To; in

Chapter

06

Conjunction
（连词）

Diagnostic Test

1. _____ well prepared you are, you still need a lot of luck in mountain climbing.

    A. However

    B. Whatever

    C. No matter

    D. Although

2. The old man asked Lucy to move to another chair _____ he wanted to sit next to his wife.

    A. because

    B. until

    C. so

    D. since

3. The artist was born poor, _____ poor he remained all his life.

    A. and

    B. or

    C. but

    D. so

4. Start out right away, _____ you'll miss the first train.

    A. and

    B. but

    C. or

    D. while

5. The incomes of skilled workers went up. _____, unskilled workers saw their earnings fall.

    A. Moreover

    B. Therefore

C. Meanwhile

D. Otherwise

6. **I'm certain David has told you his troubles, _____, it's more important to help him instead of laughing at him now.**

    A. however

    B. anyway

    C. therefore

    D. though

7. **Stand over there _____ you'll be able to see the oil painting better.**

    A. till

    B. and

    C. or

    D. but

8. **The little boy won't go sleep _____ his mother tells him a story.**

    A. or

    B. unless

    C. but

    D. whether

9. **The medicine will work more effectively _____ you drink some hot water after taking it.**

    A. as

    B. until

    C. although

    D. if

10. **She is very dear to us. We have been prepared to do _____ it takes to save her life.**

    A. however

    B. whatever

    C. whoever

    D. whichever

11. **Difficulties are nothing _____ we are not afraid of them.**

    A. for

    B. as

C. if

D. whether

12. _____ hamburgers are junk food, many children like them.

A. If

B. Unless

C. Because

D. Although

13. The form cannot be signed by anyone _____ yourself.

A. rather than

B. other than

C. more than

D. better than

14. To be great, you must be smart, confident, and, _____, honest.

A. therefore

B. above all

C. however

D. after all

15. The house was too expensive and too big. _____, I'd grown fond of our little rented house.

A. Besides

B. Therefore

C. Somehow

D. Otherwise

Knowledge Points

1. 连词是一种虚词，它不能独立担当句子成分，只起到连接词与词、短语与短语以及句子与句子的作用。在 TOEFL® Junior ™ 考试中，考查连接词的题目主要集中于对 also, however, but, therefore, although, instead 等词的辨析与使用。考查数量不多，考生在平时积累中巩固即可。

2. 连词主要分为并列连词和从属连词。

3. 并列连词表示单词、短语或句子间有并列关系。常见并列连词有：

- 表示并列关系

  and/both...and... 和

  as well as 也

  not only...but also... 不但……而且……

  neither...nor... 既不……也不……

- 表示转折关系

  but 但是

  yet 然而

  however 然而

- 表示选择关系

  either...or... 要么……要么……

  or 或者 / 否则

- 表示因果关系

  because/because of 因为

  due to/owing to/thanks to 因为，由于

  so/therefore/hence/thus 所以

  as a result 因此

  consequently/as a consequence 因此

- 表示递进关系

  in addition 另外

  furthermore 而且，此外

  again 又，此外

- 表示对比关系

  in contrast/in comparison 相比之下

  on the contrary 然而，另一方面

  while 而，然而

  nevertheless 然而

- 表示让步关系

  although/though 尽管

  even though 即使

  in spite of/despite 尽管

  regardless of 不管，除了

- 表示例证关系

  for example/for instance 例如

4. 从属连词是用以引导名词性从句、定语从句和状语从句的连词。由从属连词所引导的句子叫从句。常见从属连词有：

- that （无词义，不作成分）
- if，whether （表达是否的意义，但不作句子成分）
- 连接代词：who，whom，whose，what，which （有词义，在句子中可作主语、表语、宾语）
- 连接副词：when，where，why，how，how many，how long，how far，however，whenever，wherever （有词义，作从句的状语）

5. 需要注意的细节：

- 并列连词前后动词应保持其形式与时态一致。
- neither...nor... 或者 either...or... 的句子中谓语动词采用就近原则，与 nor 或 or 后的主语保持一致。
- not only...but also... 中的 also 有时可以省略。当 not only 放置句首时，分句要倒装。
- but 和 however 的意思相同，但是 however 后面要加逗号，but 不可以。
- because 和 so 不能同时出现在一个句子中，只能用其中的一个。
- although/though 和 but 不能同时出现在一个句子中，但是可以和 yet 同时使用。
- if 表示"是否"时，和 whether 一样。whether 后可加 or not，if 后不可以。

Assignment & Exercise

- **选词填空一：在下列空格当中填入合适的连词**

  1. We were just about ready to leave _____ it started to snow.

  2. I really want to join the hiking activity, _____ I'm too busy to go out for fun.

  3. Don't try to get off the bus _____ it has stopped.

  4. You'll miss the train _____ you hurry up.

5. We arrived at the station _____ the train had left.

6. _____ he was in poor health, he worked just as hard as everyone else.

7. Give me one more minute _____ I'll have finished.

8. Do not make the same mistake _____ I did.

9. I don't want to go out now. It is late; _____, I'm so tired that I really need a good rest.

10. I don't know _____ to go to the cinema or go to the amusement park with Nick.

- ## 选词填空二：在下列空格当中填入合适的连词

1. _____ you study hard _____ you give up the test.

2. We should pay attention _____ to industry _____ to agriculture.

3. The book is not easy. _____, it's rather difficult.

4. You can buy some fruit you like, _____, cherries or apples.

5. _____ I know he will stay here for half a year.

6. Please write me _____ you arrive in New York.

7. _____ we have satisfied you, you have no grounds of complaint.

8. It looks _____ it's going to rain.

9. We'll go and see the patient _____ we are busy.

10. The museum is _____ far _____ it will take us half an hour to get there by bus.

- 选词成句：选择合适的单词完成下列各句

1. She said she would work it out herself, _____ ask me for help.
   A. and not to
   B. but not
   C. and prefer not
   D. rather than

2. For a person with reading habits, a printed page contains not only words _____ ideas, thoughts and feelings.
   A. yet
   B. and
   C. or
   D. but

3. English is understood all over the world _____ Turkey is spoken by only a few people outside Turkey itself.
   A. while
   B. when
   C. if
   D. as

4. I asked him whether he had done all the work himself _____ whether he had had any assistance.
   A. and
   B. but
   C. nor
   D. or

5. Tom makes up his mind to get a seat for the football match _____ it means standing in a queue all night.
   A. as if
   B. as though
   C. even if
   D. whatever

6. Doing your homework is a sure way to improve your test scores, and this is especially true _____ it comes to classroom tests.

A. as

B. since

C. when

D. after

7. You may borrow this book — _____ you promise to give it back.

A. in case

B. so long as

C. as if

D. even if

8. _____ the man grew older, he lost interest in everything except gardening.

A. With

B. Since

C. While

D. As

9. _____ you understand this rule, you'll have no further difficulty.

A. Once

B. Unless

C. As

D. Until

10. I was so familiar with her that I recognized her voice _____ I picked up the phone.

A. the moment

B. after

C. before

D. while

Answers & Explanations

Diagnostic Test

1. A 题目理解为"爬山的时候，无论你准备得多好，还是需要些好运气"。however = no matter how。

2. A 题目理解为"老人请求露西挪到别的椅子上，因为他想坐在他妻子的旁边"。because 表示原因。

3. A 题目理解为"这位艺术家出身贫寒，且贫寒终生"。两个半句之间没有因果或转折关系，所以选择 and 表示并列。

4. C 题目理解为"马上出发，否则你就会错过第一班火车了"。or 表示"否则"。

5. C 题目理解为"熟练工人的收入提高了，同时，不熟练工人的收入减少了"。moreover 表示"此外"；therefore 表示"因此"；meanwhile 表示"与此同时"；otherwise 表示"否则"。

6. B 题目理解为"我确信大卫已经将他的麻烦告诉你了，不管怎么样，现在帮助他比笑话他更重要"。两个半句间没有具体的逻辑关系，anyway 表示"不管怎么样"。

7. B 题目理解为"站在那里，你就能更好地欣赏这幅油画了"。祈使句，and 表示结果。

8. B 题目理解为"这个小男孩不会睡觉，除非他的妈妈给他讲个故事"。unless 表示"除非"。

9. D 题目理解为"如果你用热水服药的话，药会更有疗效"。

10. B 题目理解为"她对我们来说太重要了。我们已经准备不惜一切代价抢救她"。whatever = everything that。

11. C 题目理解为"如果我们不怕困难，困难就什么都不是"。if 表示"如果"。

12. D 题目理解为"即使汉堡包是垃圾食品，许多孩子还是很喜欢吃"。although 表示"即使"。

13. B 题目理解为"这个表格除了你自己，任何人都不能签署"。other than 表示"除了"。

14. B 题目理解为"要想变得伟大，你必须聪明、自信，而且最主要的是诚实"。therefore 表示"因此"；above all 表示"首先；尤其是"；however 表示"然而"；after all 表示"毕竟"。

15. A 题目理解为"这个房子太贵太大了，此外，我已经越来越喜欢我们租的小房间了"。根据前后句判断出为并列关系。besides 为"此外"，表示并列；therefore 为"因此"，表示因果；somehow 为"无论如何"，表示转折；otherwise 为"除此之外"，表示转折。

选词填空一

1. when

2. but

3. before

4. unless

5. after

6. Although

7. and

8. as

9. besides

10. whether

选词填空二

1. Either; or

2. both; and

3. On the contrary

4. for example

5. So far as

6. as soon as

7. Now that

8. as if

9. even if

10. so; that

选词成句

1. D   rather than 是对称连词，表示"而不"。

2. D   not only...but (also)... 是固定搭配。

3. A   句中的并列连词 while 表示对比或相反。

4. D   只有 or 才能表示选择，表示"（是……）还是"。

5. C   even if = even though，引导的让步状语从句，表示"即使，尽管"。

6. C   when it comes to... 是固定句型，表示"当谈到……时，涉及"。题目理解为"做作业是提高考试分数的一个可靠方法，这在涉及课堂测验时尤其正确"。

7. B   so long as = as long as, 表示"只要"，题目理解为"只要你答应归还，就可以把这本书借走"。

8. D   as 引导的时间状语从句，表示事物的进展，意为"随着"，题目理解为"那人年纪越来越大，除了园艺外对其他事情都不感兴趣"。

9. A   once 引导的让步状语从句，表示"一旦"，题目理解为"一旦你明白了这条规则，就再也没有困难了"。

10. A 名词短语 the moment 用作连词，相当于 as soon as，引导时间状语从句，表示"一……就……"，类似的短语或词还有 the minute, the instance, directly, immediately 等。

Grammar

(语 法)

Diagnostic Test

1. **He had hoped _____, but he couldn't finish his thesis in time.**

    A. him to graduate this semester

    B. that he graduates this semester

    C. he would graduate this semester

    D. his graduation of this semester

2. **_____, the pay isn't attractive enough, though the job itself is quite interesting.**

    A. Generally speaking

    B. On the contrary

    C. In particular

    D. To be honest

3. **_____ a boy, the man was taken away by the police.**

    A. Supposing to murder

    B. Supposed to murder

    C. Supposing to have murdered

    D. Supposed to have murdered

4. **The computer was used in teaching. As a result, not only _____, but students became more interested in the lessons.**

    A. saved was teacher's energy

    B. was teachers' energy saved

    C. teachers' energy was saved

    D. was saved teachers' energy

5. **Only when the fire was under control _____ to return to their homes.**

    A. the residents would be permitted

    B. had the residents been permitted

C. would the residents be permitted

D. the residents had been permitted

6. **Mr. Liu took pictures and videos of many things that people _____.**

    A. had seen ago

    B. had never seen before

    C. have never seen before

    D. was not seen before

7. **We want to know _____.**

    A. when we should arrive at the airport

    B. when should we arrive at the airport

    C. when the airport we should arrive at

    D. when the airport should we arrive at

8. **He wanted to know _____ the English party.**

    A. when will we have

    B. when we will have

    C. when would we have

    D. when we would have

9. **You can't imagine _____ when they received these nice Christmas Presents.**

    A. how they were excited

    B. how excited they were

    C. how excited were they

    D. they were how excited

10. **Can you describe _____?**

    A. what your friend looks like

    B. how your friend looks like

    C. what does your friend look like

    D. how is your friend look like

11. **We will go shopping as soon as it _____.**

    A. will stop raining

    B. will stop to rain

    C. stops raining

    D. stops to rain

12. Alice has gone to the library and she didn't say _____.

A. when did she come back

B. when would she be back

C. when she come back

D. when she would be back

13. We have _____ up early in order to catch the early bus.

A. used to get

B. been used to get

C. used for getting

D. been used to getting

14. — We can use Skype to chat with each other on the Internet.

— Really? Will you please show me _____ it?

A. how to use

B. what to use

C. how can I use

D. what can I use

15. You'd better _____ too much time playing computer games.

A. don't speak

B. not to spend

C. to not spend

D. not spend

Knowledge Points

1. 三种句型

只包含一个主谓结构的句子叫做简单句 (Simple Sentences)；包含两个或两个以上主谓结构的句子叫并列复合句 (Compound Sentences)，句子与句子之间通常用并列连词或分号来连接；包含一个主句和一个或几个附属从句的句子叫主从复合句 (Complex Sentences)，从句由从属连词引导。

2. 五种基本句式和其他特殊句式

（1）主语 + 谓语 +（状语）

E.g. I work./She is crying.

- 可以作主语的成分有名词、主格代词、数词、动词不定式、动名词等。主语一般在句首。注意名词单数形式常和冠词在一起。

- 谓语由动词构成，是英语时态、语态变化的主角，一般在主语之后。谓语可以是不及物动词(vi.)，没有宾语，构成主谓结构。

（2）主语 + 系动词 + 表语

E.g. John is busy.

- 系动词（连系动词），可以是 be 动词 (am，is，are，was，were...)，或 become，turn，go，或是感官动词，如：feel，touch，hear，see 等。

- 表语：说明主语的状态、性质等。可为形容词、副词、名词、代词、不定式、分词。

（3）主语 + 谓语 + 宾语

E.g. She studies English.

- 宾语位于及物动词之后，一般同主语构成一样，不同的是构成宾语的代词必须是代词宾格，如：me，him，them 等。除了代词宾格可以作宾语外，名词、动名词、不定式等也可以作宾语。

（4）主语 + 谓语 + 宾语 + 补足语

E.g. Time would prove me right.

- 补足语放在宾语之后，用来说明宾语的状态、特征，多由名词、形容词、副词、不定式、动名词和分词充当。

（5）主语 + 谓语 + 间接宾语 + 直接宾语

E.g. My mother made me a new dress.

- 直接宾语是谓语动词的承受者，间接宾语表示谓语动作的方向（对谁做）或动作的目标（为谁做），间接宾语紧接在谓语动词后，但它不能单独存在，它和直接宾语组成双宾语。

（6）There be 句式

E.g. There is a bottle of water on the table.

- There be 句式表示"某地（或某时）有某人（或某物）"，而并非"某地（某人、某物或某时）拥有什么东西"，其形式为"There be + 代词或名词（短语）+ 地点 / 时间状语"。（其实质句式为倒装句。）这里 there 是引导词，没有词义，be 是谓语动词，代词或名词（短语）是主语。

（7）倒装句式

- 主语和谓语是句子的核心，它们之间有两种语序：一是主语在谓语之前，称为自然语序 (Natural Order)；二是主语在谓语之后，称为倒装语序 (Inverted Order)。而倒装语序中又有完全倒装 (Full Inversion) 和部分倒装 (Partial Inversion)。

- 完全倒装指将句子中的谓语全部置于主语之前。此结构通常只用于一般现在时和一般过去时。

- 部分倒装指将谓语的一部分，如助动词或情态动词置于主语之前，而谓语动词无变化。如果句中的谓语没有助动词或情态动词，则需添加助动词 do，does 或 did，并将其置于主语之前。

Assignment & Exercise

● 造句：按要求转换句型，一空一词

1. The koala comes from Australia. （变否定句）

   The koala _____ _____ from Australia.

2. He likes dolphins very much. （变一般疑问句）

   _____ he _____ dolphins very much?

3. I like Tom because he is very friendly. （对划线部分提问）

   _____ do _____ like Tom?

4. The shy girl wants to see giraffes. （对划线部分提问）

   _____ _____ does the shy girl want to see?

5. Do you have lots of clever friends? （变陈述句）

   _____ _____ lots of clever friends.

6. Pandas are from China. （同义句转换）

   Pandas _____ _____ China.

7. She doesn't want bananas at all. （变肯定句）

   She _____ bananas very _____.

8. Mr. Wu went to America by plane. （对划线部分提问）

   _____ _____ Mr. Wu go to America?

9. It took us 3 hours to go bike riding. （同义句转换）

We _____ 3 hours _____ bike riding.

10. He sometimes goes to the library. （对划线部分提问）

_____ _____ does he go to the library?

11. You mustn't talk in the reading room. （改为祈使句）

_____ _____ in the reading room.

12. I think. You won't like the film. （合并成一个句子）

I _____ think you _____ like the film.

● 翻译：根据汉语提示完成句子

1. 主谓句型：在过去的十年里，我的家乡已经发生了巨大的变化。

_____

2. 主谓句型：这种事情世界各地每天都在发生。

_____

3. 主谓宾句型：我收到了玛丽从澳大利亚寄来的信。

_____

4. 主谓宾句型：我们大家都相信杰克是一个诚实的男孩。

_____

5. 主系表句型：冬季白天短，夜晚长。

_____

6. 主系表句型：他十五岁就成为有名的钢琴家了。

　　————————————————————————————

7. 主谓双宾句型：鲁滨逊·克鲁索给自己做了一只小船。

　　————————————————————————————

8. 主谓双宾句型：这个学期我已经给父母写过三封信了。

　　————————————————————————————

9. 复合宾语句型：每天早晨我们都听到他大声朗读英语。

　　————————————————————————————

10. 我认为有可能用另一种方法解题。

　　————————————————————————————

11. 转换为 There be 句型：客人当中有两名美国人和两名法国人。

　　————————————————————————————

12. 转换为 There be 句型：从前，在海边的一个村子里住着一位老渔夫。

　　————————————————————————————

Answers & Explanations

Diagnostic Test

1. C　题目理解为"他希望能在这个学期毕业，但是他没能及时写完论文"。用虚拟语气，要加 would。

2. D　题目理解为"诚恳地说，虽然这份工作非常有趣，但是工资还不足以吸引人"。

3. D　题目理解为"这个男人被警察带走了，他被怀疑杀害了一个男孩"。"杀害了"应该是完成时的状态。

4. B 题目理解为"这台电脑被用来授课。因此，不仅可以节省老师的精力，学生们也会变得更有兴趣"。not only 可引导倒装句。

5. C 题目理解为"只有火势得到控制，居民才会被允许回到他们自己的家"。only 引导倒装句，同时，"火势得到控制"是虚拟条件，要用虚拟语气。

6. B 题目理解为"刘先生给很多东西拍摄的照片和视频都是人们从来没有见过的"。要用过去完成时。

7. A 题目理解为"我们想知道应该什么时候到机场"。用陈述语序。

8. B 题目理解为"他想知道我们什么时候办英语聚会"。用陈述语序。

9. B 题目理解为"你无法想象他们收到这些精美的圣诞礼物时是多么的兴奋"。用陈述语气。

10. A 题目理解为"你能描述一下你的朋友长什么样子吗？"用陈述语气，要用 what 来提问长相，不能用 how。

11. C 题目理解为"雨一停我们就去购物"。主句用将来时，从句要用现在时，stop doing 表示"停止正在做的事情"。

12. D 题目理解为"爱丽斯去了图书馆，没有说她什么时候回来"。用陈述语序。

13. D 题目理解为"我们现在已经习惯了早起去赶早班车"，用完成时，be used to doing 表示"习惯做某事"。

14. A 题目理解为"——我们可以用 Skype 在网上聊天。——真的吗？你能告诉我怎么用吗？"

15. D 题目理解为"你最好不要花太多时间在玩电脑游戏上"。had better not do 为固定搭配，表示"最好不要"。

造句

1. doesn't; come

2. Does; like

3. Why; you

4. What animals

5. I have

6. come from

7. wants; much

8. How did

9. spent; on

10. How often

11. Don't talk

12. don't; will

翻译

1. Great changes have taken place in my hometown in the past ten years.

2. Things of that sort are happening all over the world every day.

3. I received a letter from Mary in Australia.

4. All of us believe that Jack is an honest boy.

5. In winter, the days are short and the nights are long.

6. By the age of fifteen, he has already become a famous pianist.

7. Robinson Crusoe made himself a boat.

8. This semester I have written three letters to my parents.

9. Every morning we hear him reading English aloud.

10. I consider it possible to work out the problem in another way.

11. Among the guests, there were two Americans and two Frenchmen.

12. Once, there was an old fisherman living in a village by the sea.

Chapter 08

Adverbial Clause
（状语从句）

Diagnostic Test

1. Tom will call me as soon as he _____ home.
   A. gets
   B. has got
   C. got
   D. will get

2. We will have no water to drink _____ we don't protect the earth.
   A. until
   B. before
   C. though
   D. if

3. Everybody promises to join in the barbecue outdoors _____ it will rain that day.
   A. if
   B. as
   C. unless
   D. when

4. Relax! _____ you finish this English exam, you will be free.
   A. As well as
   B. As soon as
   C. As good as
   D. As long as

5. — So you were in the supermarket _____ you heard a strange sound, right?
   — That's true. I ran out as quickly as possible.
   A. when
   B. while

C. then

D. which

6. **The teacher speaks very loudly _____ all the students can hear her.**

A. so that

B. because

C. since

D. when

7. **— What do you think of this skirt?**

— It's beautiful and it fits me well, _____ I like it very much.

A. since

B. so

C. but

D. because

8. **_____ it snowed heavily yesterday, nobody in our class missed the lesson.**

A. Though

B. Because

C. Unless

D. Since

9. **I was drawing on the computer _____ my friend came to see me yesterday evening.**

A. before

B. after

C. while

D. when

10. **Peter likes reading newspaper _____ he is having breakfast.**

A. until

B. while

C. because

D. though

11. **Jane, please turn off the lights _____ you leave the classroom.**

A. after

B. before

C. until

D. but

12. **In summer, food goes bad easily _____ it is put in the refrigerator.**

A. until

B. if

C. unless

D. because

13. **I won't be able to understand what you say, _____ you speak too quickly.**

A. if

B. though

C. because

D. so

14. **The film "Kung Fu Panda" is _____ interesting _____ I would like to see it again.**

A. such; that

B. too; to

C. as; as

D. so; that

15. **— Your French is so good. How long have you been in France?**

— _____ I was five.

A. Until

B. Since

C. When

D. Before

Knowledge Points

状语从句在主从复合句中修饰主句中的动词、形容词或副词等。状语从句由从属连词引导，与主句连接，既可位于句首，也可位于句末。位于句首时，状语从句常用逗号与主句分开；位于句末时，其前面一般与主句连接，不用逗号分开。状语从句主要考查的类型大致如下：

状语从句分类	从句引导词	例句
时间状语从句	when, while, as, before, after, since, until, as soon as...	I was watching TV when the telephone rang.

状语从句分类	从句引导词	例句
条件状语从句	if, as long as, unless, only if...	As long as you give me the book, I will never bother you again.
原因状语从句	because, since, as, for, now that, considering that, given that...	I like swimming because it is good for my health.
目的状语从句	so that, in order that	He goes to bed early everyday so that he can get up early.
结果状语从句	so...that, such...that	It is so crowded outside that I don't want to go out.
让步状语从句	though, although, even if, even though, whatever, wherever, whenever	Wherever you go, I'll go with you.
地点状语从句	where, wherever, (anywhere, everywhere)...	This is my house where I've been living for more than twenty years.
比较状语从句	as...as..., than...	The more you exercise, the healthier you will be.
方式状语从句	as, as if, how, the way	Sometimes we teach our children the way our parents have taught us.

1. 一般情况下，时间和条件状语从句中的谓语动词用"一般现在时"表示"一般将来时"。

2. 地点状语从句一般由连接副词 where, wherever 等引导，已经形成了固定的句型，例如：
   - Where + 地点从句，there + 主句
     此句型通常译成"哪里……哪里就……"。主句在从句后面时，there 可用可不用；主句在从句的前面时，一般都不用 there。
     例如：Where there is a will, there is a way.
   - Anywhere + 地点从句 / 主句
     anywhere 本身是个副词，但常可以引导从句，相当于连词，意思类似于 wherever。anywhere 引导的从句可位于主句之前，也可以位于主句之后。而 wherever 本身就是个连词，表示"在何处，无论何处"。
     例如：Wherever the sea is, you will find seamen.

3. as 用在让步状语从句中必须倒装。

4. 比较状语从句
   - 常用引导词：as（同级比较），than（不同程度的比较）
   - 特殊引导词：the more... the more..., just as..., so..., A is to B what/as X is to Y，no... more than，not A so much as B

Assignment & Exercise

● 选词成句：选择合适的单词完成下列各句

1. I have already decided to go bike riding with you tomorrow, nothing will stop me

   (A) since
   (B) unless
   (C) when
   (D) until

   there is something urgent.

2. If it

   (A) rains
   (B) will rain
   (C) doesn't rain
   (D) won't rain

   this weekends, I will go camping with all of our classmates.

3. It was

   (A) such fine
   (B) such a fine
   (C) so fine
   (D) so fine a

   weather that they decided to go out for a picnic.

4. After finishing their education, most students would like to start to work

   (A) as soon as
   (B) so that
   (C) before
   (D) while

   they needn't depend on their parents completely.

5. If Jenny

   (A) go
   (B) goes
   (C) to go
   (D) will go

   to the concert, I will go to the concert, too.

6. We don't start the meeting

(A)	though
(B)	until
(C)	while
(D)	or

our teacher arrives.

7. I am afraid that you can't go to see the football game

(A)	since
(B)	if
(C)	unless
(D)	though

you have a ticket,

because I have only one.

8. A tourist will easily lose his way in Beijing

(A)	if
(B)	because
(C)	unless
(D)	when

he has a map or a guide.

9. We'll visit the museum this Sunday

(A)	since
(B)	if
(C)	unless
(D)	until

it rains or it's hot.

10. We'll go for a picnic if it

(A)	will rain
(B)	rains
(C)	doesn't rain
(D)	won't rain

this weekend.

11. I don't have to introduce him to you

(A)	until
(B)	unless
(C)	since
(D)	but

you know the boy.

12. My uncle has taught in this school

(A) since
(B) for
(C) until
(D) after

he was 20.

13. Remember to return the book to the school library on time,

(A) or
(B) and
(C) but
(D) then

you will be

fined.

14.

(A) Unless
(B) If
(C) Because
(D) When

you haven't finished your homework, you will not be allowed to

surf the Internet.

15. The question is

(A) very hard
(B) too difficult
(C) strange enough
(D) so strange

that nobody can answer it.

● 翻译：根据中文提示完成句子

1. 在英国，人们下车时向司机道谢是很常见的事。

_____

2. 你还记得曾经答应我只要一有空就和我去游乐园玩吗?

_____

3. 如果人们继续砍伐森林，他们将没有地方居住。

_____

4. 如果你不知道这个生词的意思，你最好查查字典。

_____

5. 我哥哥昨晚在家写电子邮件的时候，我在看电视。

_____

6. 她一到广州就会给你写信。

_____

7. 如果你现在不抓紧时间学习，就赶不上其他的同学了。

_____

8. 如果方便的话，能帮我买些水果吗？

_____

9. 在生活中，人们往往经历了才会从中吸取教训。

_____

10. 如果比尔不比以前更努力学习，他就不会进步。

_____

● 句子改错：改正使用错误的连词

1. It seemed only seconds after the boy finished washing his face.

_____

2. Let her do that, unless she will.

_____

3. Whether you stay at home. Why not do some washing?

    _____

4. I'll leave him a note such that he will know we won't come back until 11 tonight.

    _____

5. You will be late if you leave immediately.

    _____

6. You will fail in the exam if you work hard from now on.

    _____

7. If my father will come to the parent meeting or not is not known yet.

    _____

8. Where I live are there plenty of trees.

    _____

9. He will come to help you unless you phone him.

    _____

Answers & Explanations

Diagnostic Test

1. A 题目理解为"汤姆一到家就会给我打电话"。在状语从句中，主句是一般将来时，从句用一般现在时表示将来。

2. D 题目理解为"如果我们不保护地球，我们将没有水喝"。主句是一般将来时，从句用一般现在时表示将来，两句间有假设的关系。

3. C 题目理解为"每个人都答应参加户外烤肉活动，除非那天会下雨"。句子前半部分是"每个人都答应参加户外烤肉活动"，后面是"那天会下雨"，因此设空处需要连词"如果不，除非"。

4. B 题目理解为"放松点！只要英语考试一结束，你就自由了"。as well as 表示"也，同样"；as soon as 表示"一……就……"；as good as 表示"同……一样好"；as long as 表示"只要……"。

5. A 题目理解为"——那么，当你听到奇怪的声音时你在超市里，对吧？——是的，我尽快地跑了出来。"本题主要考查 when 和 while 的区别。when 既可以指一段时间，也可以指时间点，而 while 只能指一段时间，本题考查的是时间点，所以用 when。

6. A 题目理解为"老师说话的声音很大以便所有的学生都能听到"。考查连词的用法，so that 表示"以至于，以便"。

7. B 题目理解为"——你认为这条裙子怎么样？——很漂亮，很适合我，所以我很喜欢"。since 表示"既然"；so 表示"所以"；but 表示"但是"；because 表示"因为"。

8. A 题目理解为"尽管昨天雪下得很大，但我们班没有人旷课"。though 表示"尽管"；because 表示"因为"；unless 表示"除非"；since 表示"自……以来"。

9. D 题目理解为"昨天晚上朋友来看我时，我正在电脑上画画"。主句用了过去进行时，说明来的那一瞬间正在做某事，故用 when 引导时间状语从句。

10. B 题目理解为"皮特在吃早饭的时候喜欢读报纸"。while 表示"当……的时候"。

11. B 题目理解为"简，请在离开教室前关掉灯"。

12. C 题目理解为"在夏天，食品容易变坏，除非放在冰箱里"。until 表示"直到"；if 表示"如果"；unless = if...not 表示"除非"。

13. A 题目理解为"如果你说得太快，我就不能理解你说的话"。if 表示"如果；是否"；though 表示"虽然，尽管"；because 表示"因为"；so 表示"因此"。

14. D 题目理解为"《功夫熊猫》这部电影很有趣，以至于我还想再看一遍"。表示"如此……以至于……"有两种形式：such +（a/an）+ 名词 + that 或是 so + 形容词或者副词 + that。

15. B 题目理解为"——你的法语讲得真好。你来法国多久了？——从 5 岁就来了"。since 引导时间状语从句，其用法为：主句（现在完成时）+ since 从句（一般过去时）。

选词成句

1. B unless 表示"除非"，"除非有要紧事，否则任何事都不会阻挡我"。

2. C if 引导的条件状语从句，用一般现在时表将来。"去野营"应该是在不下雨的天气。

3. A weather 是不可数名词，不能用 a 修饰，故排除选项 B 和 D，such + 形容词 + 不可数名词 / 名词复数；so + 形容词 + a/an + 可数名词单数。

4. B so that 表示"为了，以便"。

5. B if 引导条件状语从句，从句用一般现在时表将来，主句仍用将来时。

6. B   not...until... 为固定搭配，表示"直到……才……"。

7. C   unless 表示"除非"。

8. C   if 表示"如果"，引导条件状语从句；because 表示"因为"，引导原因状语从句；unless 表示"除非，如果不……"，引导条件状语从句；when 表示"当……时候"，引导时间状语从句。

9. C   since 表示"自从"；if 表示"如果"；unless 表示"除非，如果不"；until 表示"直到"。

10. C 在条件状语从句中，主句用将来时，从句用一般现在时表示将来。

11. C since 表示"既然，因为"。

12. A 用于现在完成时的时间状语用 since 或 for 表达，since 后跟时间点，如 since 2006 或 since he came here；而 for 后要跟一段时间。

13. A or 表示"否则，要不然"，表示因果关系；and 表示"和"，表示并列关系；but 表示"但是"，表示转折关系；then 表示"然而"。

14. C because 表示"因为"，引导原因状语从句。

15. D so...that... 表示"如此……以至于……"。

翻译

1. It's quite common in Britain to say "Thank you" to the drivers when people get off the bus.

2. Do you still remember that you have promised me to go the amusement park with me as soon as you are free?

3. If people keep cutting down the forest, they will have nowhere to live.

4. You'd better look up the new word in a dictionary if you don't know it.

5. My brother was writing an e-mail while I was watching TV at home last night.

6. She will write to you as soon as she gets to Guangzhou.

7. If you don't make the best of your time to study, you will not catch up with others.

8. Would you buy me some fruit if it is convenient to you?

9. People usually cannot learn a lesson in life until they have actually experienced that.

10. Bill won't make any progress unless he studies harder than before.

句子改错

1. 把 after 改为 before。题目理解为"似乎仅用了几秒钟，这个男孩就洗完了脸"。before 引导时间状语从句。

2. 把 unless 改为 if。题目理解为"如果她愿意的话，就让她去做吧"。if 引导条件状语从句。在 if she will 中，will 表示愿意。

3. 把 whether 改为 since。题目理解为"既然你待在家里，为什么不洗衣服呢？" since 引导原因状语从句，语气较弱，表示已知的原因，常译为"既然"。

4. 把 such that 改为 so that。题目理解为"我会给他留下一张便条，以便让他知道我们今晚 11 点才回来"。so that 表示"以便，为了"，引导目的状语从句。

5. 把 if 改为 unless。题目理解为"除非你立即走，否则就会迟到"。

6. 把 if 改为 unless。题目理解为"除非你从现在开始努力，否则你考试会不及格"。

7. 把 if 改为 whether。题目理解为"我父亲是否来参加家长会还不能确定"。whether 和 or 连用。

8. 把 there 和 are 互换位置。题目理解为"我住的地方有许多树"。

9. 把 unless 改为 if。题目理解为"如果你给他打电话，他就会来帮助你"。

Chapter 09

Noun Clause
(名词性从句)

Diagnostic Test

1. — David, look at the man in white over there. Can you tell me _____?
    — He is a doctor.
    A. where he is
    B. who he is
    C. how he is
    D. what he is

2. — Could you tell me _____ at 10 o'clock last night?
    — Er, I was watching TV at home.
    A. what you were doing
    B. what you have done
    C. what you are doing
    D. what you did

3. I don't know the man over there. Could you tell me _____?
    A. what his name is
    B. where does he come from
    C. how old is he
    D. when did he come here

4. I want to know _____.
    A. when we should arrive at the airport
    B. when should we arrive at the airport
    C. when the airport we should arrive at
    D. when the airport should we arrive at

5. He wanted to know _____ the math examination.

A. when will we leave

B. when we will have

C. when would we have

D. when we would have

6. — Could you tell me _____?

— Fill in this form and I will give you a card.

A. how I can meet Cathy

B. where I can meet Cathy

C. when I can meet Cathy

D. whether I can meet Cathy

7. — Excuse me, can you tell me _____?

— Sorry, I'm new here.

— Thank you all the same.

A. where is the nearest hospital

B. where the nearest hospital is

C. where was the nearest hospital

D. where the nearest hospital was

8. — Do you know _____ in Australia?

— Yes. In May, 2009.

A. when Ben got his job

B. when will Ben get his job

C. when did Ben get his job

D. when Ben will get his job

9. — Can you tell me when _____?

— About two weeks ago.

A. does he buy the car

B. did he buy the car

C. he bought the car

D. he buys the car

10. — Can you tell me _____?

— By doing more speaking.

A. how I can improve my English

B. which way can I choose

C. how do I deal with my English

D. what's wrong with my English

11. — Do you know _____ the Capital Museum?

— Next Friday.

A. when will they visit

B. when they will visit

C. when did they visit

D. when they visited

12. — Could you tell me _____?

— He's in the library.

A. where Simon was

B. where is Simon

C. where was Simon

D. where Simon is

13. — Do you know _____ the girl in red is?

— You mean the girl over there? She is a nurse.

A. when

B. how

C. where

D. what

14. — Does anyone know _____?

— I hear that he was born in Sweden.

A. what he is

B. when he was born

C. where he comes from

D. which country is he from

15. — Could you tell me _____?

— Of course, last night.

A. when you reached Chengdu

B. when did you reach Chengdu

C. how you came to China

D. how did you come to China

Knowledge Points

在句子中起名词作用的句子叫名词性从句。名词性从句的功能相当于名词词组，它在复合句中能担任主语、宾语、表语、同位语、介词宾语等，因此根据它在句中不同的语法功能，名词性从句又可分别称为主语从句、宾语从句、表语从句和同位语从句。

1. 主语从句需要注意：

- 连词 that 引导主语从句时，无任何意义，也不充当任何成分，只是单纯的连词，但是通常情况下是不可以省略的。

- that 引导主语从句时，常用 it 作形式主语，而将 that 从句置于句尾。

  it 作形式主语置于句首时，常见的句型有：

  It + be + 名词 + that 从句

  It + be + 形容词 + that 从句

  It + be + 动词的过去分词 + that 从句

  It + 不及物动词 + that 从句

  It can be imagined that... 可以想象的是……

  It goes without saying that... 不用说……

  It is well-known that... 众所周知……

  It is obvious that... 显然……

  It must be admitted that... 必须承认……

- 在主语从句中用来表示惊奇、不相信、惋惜、理应如此等语气时，谓语动词要用虚拟语气 (should) + do，常用的句型有：

  It is necessary (important, natural, strange, etc.) that...

  It is suggested (requested, proposed, desired, etc.) that...

- 连接代词在句中既保留含义，又起连接作用。其作用相当于代词，在从句中充当成分。

2. 宾语从句需要注意：

- 由连接词 that 引导宾语从句时，that 在句中不作任何成分，在口语或非正式的表达中常被省略。

- 在 demand, order, suggest, decide, insist, desire, request, command, doubt 等表示要求、命令、建议、决定等意义的动词后，宾语从句常用"should + 动词原形"。

- 由 whether 或 if 引导的宾语从句需保持陈述句语序。

- who, whom, which, whose, what, when, where, why, how, whoever, whatever, whichever 等关联词引导的宾语从句相当于特殊疑问句，但是要用陈述语序。native speaker 说话时不一定会遵从陈述语序，所以口语中可以不强调使用。

- 当主句动词是现在时时，从句可根据句意使用不同时态。

- 当主句动词是过去时态（could，would 除外）时，从句则要用相应的过去时态，如一般过去时、过去进行时、过去将来时等；当从句表示的是客观真理、科学原理、自然现象时，则从句仍用现在时态。

- think，believe，suppose，expect，fancy，imagine，seem，appear 等动词后面宾语从句的否定词需要转移到主句中，即主句的谓语动词用否定式，而从句的谓语动词用肯定式。若谓语动词为 hope，宾语从句中的否定词则不能转移。

3. 表语从句需要注意：

- 引导表语从句的关联词与引导主语从句的关联词大致一样，表语从句位于连系动词后，有时用 as if 引导。

- that 引导的表语从句无任何意义，不充当任何句子成分，只是单纯的连词，通常不能省略。

4. 同位语从句需要注意：

- 可以接同位语从句的名词通常有 news，idea，fact，promise，question，doubt，thought，hope，message，suggestion，words（消息），possibility 等。

- 连词 that 引导同位语从句，通常不能省略。

- demand，wish，suggestion，resolution 等这些名词后面的同位语从句要用虚拟语气。

- 连词 whether 可以引导同位语从句，但 if 不能。

Assignment & Exercise

- 选择：从下列选项中选出正确答案

1. I hear Tom lives here, but I'm not sure

(A) which room he lives in.
(B) which room does he lives in.
(C) he lives in which room.
(D) in which room does he live.

2. I know you've got a new pen pal. I wonder

    (A) where does she live.
    (B) where she is studying.
    (C) where will she work.
    (D) where is she studying.

3. Could you please tell me

    (A) where did Carol live?
    (B) where does Carol lived?
    (C) where Carol lives?
    (D) where Carol lived?

I've lost her address.

4. My father has a computer, but he doesn't know

    (A) what
    (B) how
    (C) who
    (D) which

to use it.

5. Can you tell me

    (A) how would you help
    (B) how you helped
    (C) how you would help
    (D) how did you help

your parents at home last night?

6. I don't know

    (A) when can we hold the party
    (B) when we can hold the party
    (C) where can we hold the party
    (D) where we can hold the party

except in the classroom.

7. Your T-shirt is so cool. Could you tell me

    (A) where you buy it
    (B) where do you buy it
    (C) where you bought it
    (D) where did you buy it

?

8. You speak good English. Could you tell me

    (A) how can I improve my English
    (B) how I can improve my English
    (C) how could I improve my English
    (D) how could I improve my English

?

● 句子翻译

1. 新设计的汽车正在展出。我想知道它多少钱。

   _____

2. 每个人在社会上都扮演着重要的角色。作为社会成员，我们应尽全力去做我们应该做的。

   _____

3. 没有人能够确定 100 万年以后人类是什么样子。

   _____

4. 你能告诉我哪儿能买到有关外星人的书吗？

   _____

5. 这条狗多可爱啊！你能告诉我它是哪儿来的吗？

   _____

6. 那列火车还没到。你能告诉我火车为什么晚点吗？

   _____

● 句子改错：试判断下列连接词运用是否正确

1. Will you please tell me how can I use the electronic device?

   _____

2. The foreigners asked me what I could speak English.

   _____

3. I wonder whether you go to school on foot in all kinds of weather.

＿＿＿＿＿＿＿＿＿＿＿＿＿＿＿＿＿＿＿＿＿＿＿＿＿＿

4. It's so dark. I can't find out either it's a boy or a girl.

＿＿＿＿＿＿＿＿＿＿＿＿＿＿＿＿＿＿＿＿＿＿＿＿＿＿

5. Could you tell me if he went to Shanghai?

＿＿＿＿＿＿＿＿＿＿＿＿＿＿＿＿＿＿＿＿＿＿＿＿＿＿

6. He asked me which he could catch the early bus.

＿＿＿＿＿＿＿＿＿＿＿＿＿＿＿＿＿＿＿＿＿＿＿＿＿＿

7. Mrs. Green asked me that I would go with her.

＿＿＿＿＿＿＿＿＿＿＿＿＿＿＿＿＿＿＿＿＿＿＿＿＿＿

8. I don't know that the coat was cheap enough.

＿＿＿＿＿＿＿＿＿＿＿＿＿＿＿＿＿＿＿＿＿＿＿＿＿＿

Answers & Explanations

Diagnostic Test

1. D 题目理解为"——大卫，看那个穿白衣服的人，你能告诉我他是做什么的吗？——他是一名医生。"宾语从句用陈述语序。

2. A 题目理解为"——你能告诉我昨天晚上十点你在干什么吗？——在家看电视。"答句时态为过去进行时，故问句用过去进行时态。

3. A 题目理解为"我不认识那边的那个男士，你能告诉我他的名字吗？"疑问词 what 引导宾语从句，宾语从句应为陈述句语序。

4. A 题目理解为"我想知道我们应该什么时候到达机场"。宾语从句应使用陈述句语序。

5. D 题目理解为"他想知道我们什么时候数学考试"。宾语从句要用陈述语序，且主句用了过去时，从句也要用过去时态。

6. A 题目理解为"——你能告诉我怎样才能见到凯西吗？——填完这张表，我会给你一张卡片。"

7. B 题目理解为"——劳驾，你能告诉我最近的医院在哪儿吗？——对不起，我是新来的。——仍然谢谢你。"宾语从句应该用陈述句语序，根据语境可知用一般现在时。

8. A 题目理解为"——你知道本是什么时候在澳大利亚找到工作的吗？——知道。在2009年5月。"宾语从句要用陈述句语序。"May，2009"是过去的时间，所以用一般过去时。

9. C 题目理解为"——你能告诉我他什么时候买的车吗？——大约两周前。"tell后面跟了双宾语，由when引导的从句作tell的宾语，宾语从句要用陈述句语序，且根据答语的时间是两周前，所以用一般过去时。

10. A 题目理解为"——你能告诉我怎样提高英语水平吗？——要多练习口语。"宾语从句用陈述句语序。

11. B 题目理解为"——你知道他们什么时候去参观首都博物馆吗？——下周五。"根据答语中的时间状语可知宾语从句用一般将来时，再根据宾语从句需用陈述句语序可知选B。

12. D 题目理解为"——你能告诉我西蒙在哪儿吗？——他在图书馆。"宾语从句的语序为陈述语序。此处的could为委婉语气而非过去时。

13. D 题目理解为"——你知道那个穿红衣服的女孩是做什么的吗？——是那边的那个女孩么？她是一名护士。"通过答句可知前一句是问职业，因此用what提问。

14. C 题目理解为"——有人知道他来自哪里吗？——我听说他出生在瑞典。"本句是含有特殊疑问词的宾语从句，根据宾语从句的语法规则和上下文的语境可知答案应选C。

15. A 题目理解为"——你能告诉我你是什么时候到达成都的吗？——可以，昨天晚上。"根据答语last night可知要用when引导宾语从句，而且宾语从句要用陈述语序。

选择

1. A 题目理解为"我听说汤姆住在这儿，可是我不确定他住在哪个房间"。宾语从句要用陈述语序，此处which room作为先行词，后面用陈述句。

2. B 题目理解为"听说你有了新笔友，我想知道她在哪儿学习"。宾语从句必须是陈述语序，即"连接词+主语+谓语+其他成分"。

3. C 题目理解为"你能告诉我卡罗尔住在哪儿吗？我把她的地址弄丢了"。此句考查宾语从句，要用陈述语序。另外，这是一个非常婉转的请求句，要用一般现在时。

4. B 题目理解为"我父亲有一台电脑，但他不知道怎么用"。这里考查宾语从句，"疑问词+不定式"作宾语。

5. B 题目理解为"你能告诉我你昨晚在家是怎样帮助父母的吗？"宾语从句要用陈述语序，根据句尾的时间状语 last night 可知应该用一般过去时。

6. D 题目理解为"我不知道除了教室之外我们还能在哪里开派对"。根据句意，这里表示举行聚会的地点，排除选项 A 和 B；宾语从句要用陈述句语序。

7. C 题目理解为"你的 T 恤太酷了，能告诉我在哪里买的吗？"宾语从句的语序应为陈述语序，由句意可判断时态应为一般过去时。

8. B 题目理解为"你英语讲得不错，你能告诉我怎样才能提高英语水平吗？"根据宾语从句的语法规则，从句要用陈述语序，此句时态要用一般现在时。

句子翻译

1. The newly-designed car is on show now. I wonder how much it costs.

2. Everyone plays an important role in society. As members, we should try our best to do what we should do.

3. No one can be sure what man will look like in a million years.

4. Could you tell me where I can buy the books about aliens?

5. How lovely the dog is! Can you tell me where you got it?

6. The train hasn't arrived yet. Could you tell me why the train is late?

句子改错

1. 把 how can I use 改为 how to use

2. 把 what 改为 if

3. 把 whether 改成 how

4. 把 either 改为 whether

5. 把 went 改为 has gone

6. 把 which 改为 if

7. 把 that 改为 whether

8. 把 that...was 改为 if...is

Chapter 10

10

Attributive Clause
（定语从句）

Diagnostic Test

1. Is this the room _____ I can live?

   A. which

   B. in which

   C. that

   D. the one

2. The police caught the man _____ stole a computer in our school.

   A. whom

   B. who

   C. whose

   D. which

3. We will never forget the day _____ we spent whole day getting together.

   A. when

   B. that

   C. which

   D. what

4. His father showed us around the factory _____ he has worked for about 20 years.

   A. which

   B. that

   C. why

   D. where

5. Bob, I'll go and help my parents on the farm. Please look after my little sister and the dog _____ are at home.

   A. that

   B. which

C. who

D. whom

6. **I have already read the first book _____ you lent me yesterday.**

   A. where

   B. when

   C. which

   D. that

7. **The city _____ we visited a few years ago is more beautiful than before.**

   A. where

   B. which

   C. it

   D. when

8. **This is our house _____ we have lived for ten years.**

   A. which

   B. when

   C. that

   D. where

9. **Children like something _____ are made in different colors.**

   A. they

   B. it

   C. that

   D. which

10. **—What are you talking about?**

    —We're talking about the teacher and his school _____ we visited yesterday.

    A. which

    B. whom

    C. who

    D. that

11. **The woman _____ is a friend of mine.**

    A. who I had a talk

    B. whom I had a talk with

C. which I had a talk with

D. whom I had a talk

12. **I love the village _____ the people are really friendly.**

A. that

B. which

C. where

D. who

13. **—I don't know your brother.**

—Oh. The man _____ came to see me yesterday is my brother.

A. who

B. whose

C. where

D. whom

14. **Would you please tell us _____ we can drive a car?**

A. what

B. how

C. who

D. which

15. **The young man _____ on the Internet is my oral English teacher.**

A. who I had a chat

B. whom I had a chat with

C. whom I had a chat

D. which I had a chat with

Knowledge Points

1. 定语从句在句中作定语，修饰名词或代词，被修饰的名词、词组或代词即先行词。定语从句通常出现在先行词之后，由关系词（关系代词或关系副词）引出。

2. 定语从句中 that 与 which 的关系

● 关系代词在定语从句中作表语，不管是人或物只能用 that。

- 当先行词是 all, something, anything, nothing, everything, little, much, the one, none 等时，引导定语从句多用关系代词 that。
- 当定语从句所修饰的先行词为物时，关系代词可用 which 或 that，当先行词既指物又指人时，多用 that 引导。
- 当先行词被形容词的最高级修饰时，引导定语从句的关系代词只能用 that，而不能用 which。
- 当先行词为 the only, the very, the first, the last, few, little, no, all, one of, the same 等修饰时，须用关系代词 that 来引导。
- 当主句中已有疑问词 who 或 which 时，要用关系代词 that。
- 在介词后面的关系代词只能用 which。
- 在非限定性定语从句中不能用 that。

3. 定语从句需要注意：

- 关系副词 when, where, why 的含义相当于"介词 + which"结构，可以互换。
- that 可以用在表示时间、地点、理由、方式的名词后，取代 when, where, why 和"介词 + which"引导的定语从句。在口语中 that 常被省略。

Assignment & Exercise

- 选词成句：选择合适的单词填入下列空格中

1. Have you found the answer to the question _____ (that, what) I asked you this morning?

2. There are lots of things _____ (whose, that) I need to prepare before the trip.

3. The most important thing that we should think about is _____ (that, what) we should do next.

4. The girl _____ (who, whom) won the gold medal comes from Beijing Sunshine Secondary School.

5. Have you found the information about the famous people _____ (what, which) you can use for the report?

6. Jamie is a young cook _____ (who, whom) wants to improve school dinners.

7. I still remember the park _____ (that, where) we first met.

8. I enjoy reading in the library _____ (where, which) I lose myself in a world of good books.

9. Mary found her bike _____ (which, what) she lost a week ago.

10. Scientists have made a new computer program _____ (which, what) allows the computer to cry out for help if someone has stolen it.

11. He told everything _____ (which, that) he knew about the accident.

12. They talked of the things and people _____ (who, that) they remembered.

13. Jim dislikes people _____ (whom, who) talk much but never do anything.

14. He lived in a small village, _____ (which, where) was a long way from the railway station.

15. Do you remember the boy _____ (who, whose) mother works in our school?

● 排序：根据中文提示给下列词语排序，组成正确的句子

1. 我讨厌那种说得多做得少的人。
   hate people   I   but   talk much   who   do little

   _____

2. 他是这家工厂中有经验的工程师之一，他的努力工作被众人赏识。
   in this factory   he is   whose   hard work   was appreciated by others   one of the
   experienced engineers

   _____

3. 他昨天买的书十分有趣。
   yesterday   very interesting   is   he bought   the book

   _____

4. 昨天我们遇见的那位年轻女士是我们的新数学老师。

whom　our new Math teacher　the young lady　yesterday　is　we met

_____

5. 没人知道她没来开会的原因。

the meeting　knows　the reason why　nobody　she didn't　come to

_____

6. 月球是个没有生命的世界。

a world　is　the moon　no life　there　is　where

_____

7. 他忘记了自己什么时候到的机场。

he arrived at the airport　has　he　the time　forgotten　when

_____

8. 他还记得和你全家一起度过的那些天。

still　he　that　remembers　with your family　the days　he spent

_____

9. 他到了小时候全家曾经住过的村庄。

he　his family　the village　got to　when he was a child　where　once lived

_____

10. 这些钱将会被用来帮助在海啸中失去家园的人们。

the money　who　in the Tsunami　used to　will be　help the people　lost their
homes

_____

● 句子填空：在空格内填入合适的词

1. He lost the money _____ he would pay for his education.

2. All _____ I want badly is a new sports car.

3. A survey was carried out on the death rate of newly-born babies in that region, the results of _____ were surprising.

4. Charlie Chaplin, _____ was born in 1889, is one of the greatest actors in the history of cinema.

5. _____ is mentioned above, the number of students in senior high schools is increasing.

6. Recently I bought an ancient Chinese vase, the price of _____ was very reasonable.

7. She found her calculator _____ she lost it.

8. In Shanghai, many tall buildings have been put up _____ there used to be poor old houses.

9. He's got himself into a dangerous situation _____ he is likely to lose control over the plane.

10. I can think of many cases _____ students obviously knew a lot of English words and expressions but couldn't write good essays.

11. American women usually identify their friends as someone with _____ they can talk frequently.

12. I like places _____ it's not cold in winter.

13. In the dark street, there wasn't a single person to _____ she could turn for help.

14. Pass me the book _____ cover is red.

Answers & Explanations

Diagnostic Test

1. B 题目理解为"这是我能住的房间吗？"先行词 room 表示地点，带入从句后在从句中作地点状语。

2. B 题目理解为"警察抓到了在我们学校偷电脑的那个人"。先行词 man 表示人，带入定语从句后在从句中作主语。

3. A 题目理解为"我们都不会忘记我们一起度过的那一天"。先行词为 day，在从句中作状语。

4. D 题目理解为"他的父亲带我们参观了他工作了 20 年的工厂"。引导词为 where。

5. A 题目理解为"鲍勃，我去农场帮父母干活，请照顾我在家的小妹妹和狗"。先行词 little sister and the dog 指的是人和物，引导词只能用 that。

6. D 题目理解为"昨天我已经读了你借给我的第一本书"。当先行词前有序数词修饰时，定语从句的引导词用 that。

7. B 题目理解为"我们几年前参观的城市现在变得更漂亮了"。定语从句的引导词在从句中作宾语，因此用 which。

8. D 题目理解为"这是我们住了十年的房子"。引导词 where 在从句中作地点状语。

9. C 题目理解为"孩子们喜欢五颜六色的东西"。先行词是不定代词时，定语从句的引导词用 that。

10. D 题目理解为"——你们在谈论什么？——我们在谈论我们昨天拜访的老师和他的学校"。先行词既有人又有物时，定语从句的引导词用 that。

11. B 题目理解为"同我说话的女人是我的朋友"。先行词是人，talk with sb，因此用 whom 引导。

12. C 题目理解为"我喜欢那个村子，村民都很友好"。引导词 where 在从句中作地点状语。

13. A 题目理解为"——我不认识你的兄弟。——哦。昨天来看我的那个人就是我的兄弟。"先行词 man 是人，在从句中作主语，因此用 who。

14. B 题目理解为"你能告诉我们怎样开车吗？"后面的从句主谓宾齐全，因此引导词用 how，在从句中作状语。

15. B 题目理解为"和我在网上聊天的那个年轻人是我的口语老师"。先行词是人，作 chat with 的宾语。

选词成句

1. that 先行词是物，引导词用 that。

2. that 先行词 things 为物，引导词用 that。

3. what 由 what 引导名词性从句，what 为 do 的宾语。

4. who 先行词为人，在从句中作主语，故只能用 who，而不能用 whom。

5. which 先行词为 information，famous people 用于修饰 information，关系词用 which。

6. who 先行词 cook 指人，关系代词在定语从句中作主语，也指代人。

7. where 先行词是 park，在定语从句中作地点状语，故用关系副词 where。

8. where 先行词 in the library 表示地点，用关系副词 where。

9. which 先行词是 her bike，在从句中作 lost 的宾语。

10. which 先行词是 program，在从句中作主语。

11. that 当先行词是 everything 的时候，关系代词用 that。

12. that 当先行词既有人又有物时，关系代词用 that。

13. who 关系代词在定语从句中作主语。

14. which 先行词 village 虽为地点名词，但在定语从句中作主语。

15. whose mother 与 the boy 构成所属关系。

排序

1. I hate people who talk much but do little.

2. He is one of the experienced engineers in this factory whose hard work was appreciated by others.

3. The book he bought yesterday is very interesting.

4. The young lady whom we met yesterday is our new Math teacher.

5. Nobody knows the reason why she didn't come to the meeting.

6. The moon is a world where there is no life.

7. He has forgotten the time when he arrived at the airport.

8. He still remembers the days that he spent with your family.

9. He got to the village where his family once lived when he was a child.

10. The money will be used to help the people who lost their homes in the Tsunami.

句子填空

1. which/that/不填 先行词为 money 指代物，关系词在从句中作宾语，引导词用 which 或 that 或省略。

2. that/不填 从句缺少宾语，All 为不定代词，引导词用 that 或省略。

3. which 非限定性定语从句，从句缺主语。

4. who 先行词指代人，为从句主语，因此引导词用 who。

5. As as 引导定语从句，译为"就像……那样，正如所……的"。

6. which 非限定性定语从句引导词用 which，如果修饰 price 应该用 whose。

7.　where　从句的成分齐全，所以不是定语从句，故引导词用 where，引导地点状语从句。

8.　where　从句中的成分齐全，所以不是定语从句，where 引导地点状语从句。

9.　where　先行词为 situation，从句是完整的句子，where 在从句中作地点状语。

10.　where　case 为抽象地点名词，从句是完整的句子，where 在从句中作地点状语。

11.　whom　此处的固定搭配是 talk with sb.，that 不能和介词连用。

12.　where　先行词 place 表示地点，从句为完整的句子，where 在从句中作地点状语。

13.　whom　turn to sb. 意为"向某人寻求帮助"，that 不能和介词连用。

14.　whose　定语从句中 whose 修饰 cover。

Practice

(练 习)

Practice Set 1

Questions 1~8 refer to the following article from a magazine.

1.   Mary Donaldson

(A) is worried
(B) is worry
(C) worrying
(D) worried

about her 16-year-old daughter, Sophia. Six months

ago, Sophia came back from a party, upset and unhappy. From then

2.   on, she thought of

(A) anything but
(B) everything about
(C) something about
(D) nothing but

how to lose weight and become

3.   beautiful. She refused to eat and

(A) kept in doing
(B) kept on doing
(C) kept do
(D) kept doing

exercise. Sophia had always

been a little heavy, so when she decided to go on a diet,

4.   Mary

(A) encouraged
(B) praised
(C) blamed
(D) criticized

her. She felt that her daughter would look more

5. attractive if she lost 10 kilograms.

(A) But,
(B) So,
(C) Because,
(D) However,

Sophia has lost over 20 kilograms

up to now and she is too thin and sick. But Sophia thinks that she is still

6. too heavy and refuses to start eating as usual. Sophia's mind

(A) is full of
(B) is fill of
(C) is full with
(D) is fill with

the

idea of losing weight. Mary regrets she has encouraged her daughter at first,

7. because Sophia is

(A) only
(B) not only
(C) no longer
(D) not longer

satisfied with her figure. Mary tries to tell Sophia

that true beauty comes from within. The most ordinary face becomes

8. beautiful

(A) when
(B) until
(C) while
(D) till

the person behind it is filled with confidence, wisdom and the

joy of life.

Questions 1~8 refer to the following article from a magazine.

1.   In the past
   (A) few
   (B) a few
   (C) little
   (D) a little
years, human have begun destroying rainforests in

search of three major resources: land for crops, wood for paper and other products,

2.   land for
   (A) raise
   (B) raises
   (C) raised
   (D) raising
farm animals. The action affects the environment

3.
   (A) as a whole.
   (B) as a fact.
   (C) as a matter.
   (D) as a result.
For example, a lot of carbon dioxide in the air comes

4.   from burning the rainforests. People
   (A) obviously
   (B) clearly
   (C) surprisingly
   (D) extremely
have a need for what we

5.   gain from cutting trees
   (A) and
   (B) but
   (C) so
   (D) because
we will suffer much more than we will

6.   benefit.
   (A) When people cut down trees,
   (B) When trees cut down by people,
   (C) Being cut down by people,
   (D) To cut down tress,
generally they can only use the land

for a year or two. Rainforests are often called the world's drug store. More than 25% of the

medicines we use today come from plants in rainforests. However, fewer than 1%

7.   of rainforest plants

(A) have been examined
(B) have examined
(C) had been examined
(D) had examined

for their medical value. It is extremely

likely that our best chance to cure diseases lies somewhere in the

8.   world's

(A) shrinking
(B) shrinked
(C) expanding
(D) expanded

rainforests.

Questions 1~8 refer to the following article from a newspaper.

1. Animals are everywhere,

    (A) but
    (B) and
    (C) also
    (D) or

    could the secret of understanding them be beyond

human's perception? Well perhaps, because there is a strong evolutionary

2. link

    (A) among
    (B) amongst
    (C) between
    (D) in

    the animals responding and sensing to disasters in advance like

getting out of the way, but we have no idea that how they are doing this.

3. The belief

    (A) that
    (B) of
    (C) what
    (D) which

    animals can predict earthquake has been around for

4. centuries. Catfish moving violently, chickens that stop

    (A) lie
    (B) lay
    (C) lying
    (D) laying

    eggs and bees

5.

    (A) leave
    (B) leaving
    (C) to leave
    (D) be left

    their hive in a panic have been reported. But precisely what animals'

6. sense,

(A) about they feel anything at all,

(B) if they feel anything at all,

(C) whether they feel nothing at all,

(D) when they feel nothing at all,

is a mystery. One theory is that wild

and domestic creatures feel the Earth vibrate before humans. Other ideas suggest

7. they detect electrical changes in the air or gas

(A) releasing

(B) released

(C) being releasing

(D) being released

from the Earth.

Some creatures, for instance, may be able to "hear" infrasound—sounds

8. produced by natural phenomena,

(A) including

(B) excluding

(C) concluding

(D) precluding

earthquake, volcanoes, and storms,

that are inaudible to the human ear. This ability may give these animals enough time to

react and flee to safety.

Practice Set 4

Questions 1~4 refer to the following article from school newspapers.

This week we asked Li Ping, our champion on the newly English competition

1. about the best way to learn English. When

(A) being asked
(B) asked
(C) asking
(D) is asked

about studying

grammar, she said, "Studying grammar was a great way to learn a language.

2. But it is too

(A) boring.
(B) bored.
(C) interested.
(D) interesting.

I'd like to read English magazines." She also

3. thought that watching English movies was a good way too

(A) because
(B) so
(C) and
(D) that

she could listen

to the actors saying the words. Besides, she also said that joining the English

4. corner was the best way to improve her English. She added that

(A) chatting
(B) to chat
(C) to chatting
(D) chat

with

classmates was not helpful at all because you cannot avoid using Chinese.

Questions 5~10 refer to the following article.

Long long ago, man had only the sun and the moon for light. After they learned

5. to

(A) make
(B) do
(C) take
(D) find

fire, they carried burning sticks to light their way. Later they

6. learned to

(A) come
(B) go
(C) put
(D) take

sticks into fat. The burning fat had a brighter light and

7.

(A) stayed
(B) worked
(C) made
(D) lasted

longer. After man learned to use a wick, they invented candles,

8.

(A) what
(B) who
(C) which
(D) why

were improved as time went by. People still use candles today. Later man

made many kinds of oil lamps. These lamps burned coal oil and had

9. glass chimneys. Later the gas light which needed

(A) neither
(B) either
(C) both
(D) all

wicks nor chimneys was

developed. All these lights had one thing in common—they had to be

10. lighted

(A) as
(B) like
(C) with
(D) without

a fire. In 1879, Thomas Edison invented the light bulb. It can be

lighted without a fire.

Questions 1~4 refer to the following e-mail.

Dear Lisa,

1. How can I ever thank you for the awesome basketball shoes you [____] me for

(A) gave
(B) give
(C) given
(D) have give

my birthday? It's one of the most beautiful Kobe Bryant shoes that I've

2. seen, and I am so grateful to have it. I've [____] worn it several times, and

(A) already
(B) ever
(C) never
(D) yet

received many complements. Thanks to the shoes, I can bounce higher and

3. play smoother. It's great to have friends like you [____] understand my

(A) whom
(B) which
(C) who
(D) that

4. passion. Thanks for making this birthday [____] a memorable one.

(A) so
(B) such
(C) too
(D) more

Questions 5~10 refer to the following article from a newspaper.

5.　Today more people are using refrigerators. Some are big,

(A) other
(B) the other
(C) others
(D) another

are small.

Compared with big ones, the small ones have only one door and can only

6.

(A) keep
(B) prevent
(C) change
(D) avoid

things cold and fresh. And they cannot even make ice and freeze

7.　food. There are

(A) that refrigerators also
(B) also refrigerators that
(C) also being that refrigerators
(D) the refrigerators that also

are friendly to the environment. In the

1970s, the world was in energy crisis. Refrigerators used too much energy. So

8.　people began to

(A) think of
(B) care for
(C) care about
(D) think out

ways to improve it. At last, a kind of new

refrigerators was made. They use very little energy, but they are too expensive. They

9.　cost twice or three

(A) times as than
(B) times few than
(C) times much than
(D) times more than

the ones that we use at home. However,

people believe that kind of refrigerators will be cheaper and cheaper.

10.

(A) As a result,
(B) As a matter,
(C) As a fact,
(D) As a cause,

they will be more and more popular.

Practice Set 6

Questions 1~4 refer to the following announcement.

Dear students,

Do you know that up to 70% of trash from a school like ours is paper that can be

1. recycled? Our recycling efforts are important to help

(A) saving
(B) to save
(C) save
(D) saved

the wood

consumption and protect our environment. We suggest that everyone of you

2.

(A) getting involved in
(B) get involved in
(C) get involving in
(D) to get involved in

implementing a new recycling program. And we encourage

3. you to reuse the textbooks and donate your books to our library.

(A) However,
(B) In addition,
(C) In addition to,
(D) But,

4. we hope you can try to

(A) take use of
(B) take advantage of
(C) make up for
(D) take account of

the recycling containers in every

classroom. Thank you for your attention and participation.

A poor man, who could read a little, found one old book someday. It was a thin strip of

5.　vellum
(A) on which
(B) in which
(C) at which
(D) above which

was written the secret of the "Touchstone"! The touchstone

6.　was a small pebble that could turn any common metal
(A) in
(B) into
(C) on
(D) to

pure gold. The

writing explained that it was lying among thousands of other pebbles that looked

7.　exactly like it. But the secret was that the real stone would feel warm,
(A) while
(B) when
(C) and
(D) since

ordinary pebbles were cold. So the man camped on the seashore and began to testing

8.　pebbles. When he felt one that was cold, he threw it into the sea
(A) in order not to
(B) in order to
(C) so that
(D) so as to

9.　pick up the same pebbles hundreds of times. He spent a whole day
(A) do
(B) doing
(C) did
(D) does

10.　this but none of them was the touchstone.
(A) Fortunate,
(B) Fortunately,
(C) It is fortunate,
(D) Being fortunate,

about mid-afternoon, he

picked up a pebble and it was warm. But he threw it into the sea

11. before he realized what he

(A) have done.
(B) had done.
(C) was doing.
(D) did.

He had formed a strong habit of

12. throwing each peddle into the sea. So it is with opportunity.

(A) Unless
(B) Only
(C) If
(D) Until

we are careful,

it's easy to fail to recognize an opportunity when it is in hand.

Answers & Explanations

Practice Set 1

1. A 词组搭配记忆：be worried about = worry about，表示"担忧，担心"。

2. D nothing but 表示"只有……"的意思；anything but 表示"绝对不"。"她只关心减肥和变得漂亮"，所以排除 everything 和 something。

3. D 固定搭配：keep doing sth. 表示"坚持做某事，持续做某事"的意思；keep on doing sth. 表示"继续做某事"。

4. A 从选项后一句 She felt that her daughter would look more attractive if she lost 10 kilograms. 考生可推断玛丽最开始应该是鼓励女儿减肥的。encourage 表示"鼓励"；praise 表示"表扬"；blame 表示"责备"；criticize 表示"批评"。

5. D 玛丽觉得索菲娅减掉 10 公斤就会很好，结果索菲娅减掉了 20 公斤。中间需要填的应该是表转折的词。but，however 皆表示"但是"的意思，但是 but 后面不可以加逗号。

6. A be full of = be filled with，表示"充满的，装满的"。

7. C "玛丽为最开始鼓励女儿减肥的事情感到后悔，因为女儿……满意自己的身材"，可以推断出应该是女儿不再满意，no longer 表示"不再"。

8. A 句意理解为"当人有了自信、智慧和快乐，他/她才会变得美丽"，until 和 till 是"直到……的时候"，while 强调动作的持续进行，与题意矛盾，故选 A。

Practice Set 2

1. A   in the past few years/days 为固定说法，表示"过去几年 / 过去几天里"，用于现在完成时态。few 和 a few 后加可数名词，little 和 a little 后加不可数名词。

2. D   land for... 中 for 为介词，后面加动名词形式。

3. A   as a whole 表示"整体，整个"的意思。

4. A   人们有需求是很明显的，所以正确答案为 obviously。

5. B   选项前后不存在因果关系，故排除选项 C 和 D。后面 we will suffer much more than we will benefit 明显与前面表达的意思不一样，所以正确答案为 B。

6. A   选项部分为时间状语从句，主句是"他们只能用一两年土地"，从句表达的应该是"人们砍树"，主语应该是人。

7. A   植物被检测，要用被动形式，排除选项 B 和 D，全文用的都是一般现在时，故排除选项 C。

8. A   按照全文的意思，热带雨林是逐渐缩减的，故排除选项 C 和 D。动词 ing 形式可作形容词修饰名词。

Practice Set 3

1. A   根据上下文可知，前后两句为转折关系，选 but。

2. C   between 常指"在……（两者）之间"，among 和 amongst 用于指"在……（三者或三者以上）之间"。

3. A   此题考查同位语从句。

4. D   lay eggs 是下蛋的意思，stop + doing 形式表示"停止正在做的某事"。

5. B   通过 and 可以推断整句为并列句，动词形式要一致，前面是 laying，后面应该是 leaving。

6. B   由全文得知，动物是有些感受的，不是 feel nothing，故排除选项 C 和 D。选项 B 可理解为"是否真的有某些感受"，表示"是否"用 if。

7. B   gas 是被释放出去的，所以选择过去分词，排除选项 A 和 C，没有强调"正在"，排除选项 D。

8. A   natural phenomena 包括地震、火山喷发、风暴等。including 表示"包括"；excluding 表示"排除"；concluding 表示"结束，推断"；precluding 表示"阻止，排除"。

Practice Set 4

1. B   when...about studying grammar 为插入语，作状语，后面 she 作主语，said 作谓语。由此推断她是被问到关于学习语法的问题。过去分词 asked 表被动，相当于 when she was asked about...。

2. A   Studying grammar was a great way to learn a language. 这句话说的是"学习语法是学习一门语言的好方法"，之后出现 but 表转折，因此不可能是"有趣"，所以排除选项 C 和 D。形容人用形容词 ed 形式，形容物用形容词 ing 形式，故选 A。

3. A 通过整句话，可以推断出 watching English movies was a good way 和后面的 she could listen to the actors saying the words 有一定的因果关系，是因为"能听演员说台词"，所以"能学到英语"，由此可以得出"通过看电影可以学习英语"，所以选择 because。

4. A she added that 中 that 引导宾语从句，说明选项以后应为一个完整的句子。...with classmates was not helpful at all 有 was 充当谓语成分，可以直接判断 ...with classmates 充当主语成分，动词作主语需要用动名词形式。

5. A make fire 表示"生火"。

6. C put...into... 表示"把……插入……里"。此句译为"后来他们学会把木棍插入油脂里"。come into 表示"进来"；go into 表示"从事；调查"。

7. D 该句理解为"油脂燃烧发出的光更明亮且持续时间更长。"stay 表示"停留，逗留，留下"；work 表示"工作"；make 表示"使……"；last 表示"持续，延续"。

8. C 此句为非限定性定语从句，用关系代词 which 引导。

9. A 选项后出现 nor，可直接得出答案为 A。neither...nor...，表示"既不……也不……"；either...or... 表示"或……或……"。

10. C 句子理解为"……他们都要用火来点燃"。在四个选项中只有 with 表示"以某种方式，用……"。

Practice Set 5

1. A 篮球鞋是过去送的，句子前后没有表示完成时态的标志词，所以选择动词过去式。

2. A 这句话要表达的意思是"我穿过这双篮球鞋，并且得到了很多赞美"，所以表示的是"已经穿上了"，"已经"是 already。

3. C you 后面的词引导了修饰 you 的一个从句，可以排除 which。从句缺主语，that 不能用作主语，whom 为宾格形式也不能用作主语，所以正确答案为 who。

4. B 选项后面是 a memorable one，只有 such 后面可以修饰名词，选项 A、C、D 后面要修饰形容词或副词。

5. C 选项前后并列，some 和 others 连用，one 和 the other 连用。other 可作形容词或代词，表示"别的，其他的"，another 泛指"另一个，又一个，再一个"。

6. A refrigerator 的意思是"冰箱"，其作用是"保持"食物冷冻且新鲜。prevent 表示"预防"；change 表示"改变"；avoid 表示"避免"。

7. B 首先确定 also 的位置。该句所要表达的意思是"也有的冰箱是有利于环境的"，排除选项 A 和 D。that 应该引导后面的 are friendly to the environment 来修饰 refrigerators。

8. A think of 表示"想到，想起，考虑"；care for 表示"照顾，喜欢"；care about 表示"关注"；think out 表示"想出，想清楚"。

9. D 用倍数比较的时候用"基数词 + times + 形容词比较级 + than"。

10. A as a result 表示"结果"。

Practice Set 6

1. C help 后面需要加动词原形。

2. B get involved in 表示"参与"的意思，可以排除 C 选项。suggest 接宾语从句用 should do 的虚拟语气形式，should 可以省略，故选 B。

3. B 首先判断句子前后不存在转折关系，排除选项 A 和 D。in addition 和 in addition to 都表示"还有"的意思，前者相当于副词，通常放在句首，后面接完整句子；后者相当于介词，to 后边要接宾语。

4. B take advantage of 表示"利用"的意思，相当于 make use of。make up for 表示"弥补"的意思；take account of 表示"顾及"的意思。

5. A vellum 是"羊皮卷"的意思，在羊皮卷上写着 touchstone 的秘密，"在……之上"用 on which。

6. B 固定搭配 turn into 表示"把……变成……"。turn in 表示"上交"；turn on 表示"接通；打开"；turn to 表示"求助于；求教；查阅"。

7. A the real stone would feel warm 和 ordinary pebbles were cold 形成对比关系，while 作并列连词用，意思为"而，然而"，表示对比。

8. A "他把冰凉的卵石扔进海里是为了不想多次捡到同一块"，"为了不做某事"是 in order not to do sth.。

9. B 固定搭配：spend + 时间 + (on) doing sth.，意思是"花费时间做某事"。

10. B 该题考查副词作状语，fortunate 为形容词，加 ly 变成副词 fortunately，意思是"幸运地"。

11. B 这篇文章用过去式，此处强调过去的完成状态，故用过去完成时。

12. A 后半句表达的意思是"机会在手很难发现"，前边的条件应该是"除非我们认真一些"，故选择 unless。

Practice Set 1

Questions 1~4 refer to the following note.

Dear Michael,

I am very excited to know that you are going to organize a field trip for the class.

1.   Mr. Philip told me that and

   (A)   me asked to help
   (B)   asked to help me
   (C)   asked me to help
   (D)   asked me help

you with the detailed

2.   arrangement. I've already made it and leave it here. Since we will

   (A)   set out
   (B)   set to
   (C)   set for
   (D)   set at

3.   after finishing the final test, we don't have too much time on discussing it. I will

appreciate it very much

   (A)   when
   (B)   while
   (C)   if
   (D)   whether

you could contact me and tell me

4.   your plan

   (A)   so what
   (B)   so that
   (C)   in order to
   (D)   if

I can make a plan report before next Wednesday.

Yours,
Linda

Questions 5~8 refer to the following announcement.

Dear students,

5.

| (A) Since |
| (B) Because of |
| (C) When |
| (D) While |

our school is going to rebuild our dining hall, we are going to

collect your ideas or suggestions on the construction of the dining hall.

6. Everyone could write

| (A) something |
| (B) anything |
| (C) all |
| (D) both |

you want, for example, to reduce the price, to

add flavored snacks, to set slot machines and so on.

7.

| (A) There are a letter box |
| (B) There have a letter box |
| (C) There has a letter box |
| (D) There is a letter box |

in the front door of the dormitory building, and you

8. can put your ideas into it. We are

| (A) looking forward to |
| (B) looked forward to |
| (C) having looked forward to |
| (D) having been looked forward to |

them.

Thank you for your participation.

Best Regards,
The Student Union

Questions 9~12 refer to the following announcement.

Our school will decide to discontinue its free bus service for students.

9.   The reason

    (A) given
    (B) giving
    (C) is giving
    (D) is given

for this decision is that

10.

    (A) some
    (B) any
    (C) few
    (D) little

students ride the buses and the buses are expensive to operate. Currently, the

buses run from the center of campus and through some of the

11.   neighborhoods

    (A) surround
    (B) surrounded
    (C) surrounding
    (D) is surrounding

the campus. The money saved by eliminating the

bus service will be used to expand the overcrowded

12.   student parking lots.

    (A) If you have any questions or suggestions
    (B) You have any questions and suggestions if
    (C) If any questions and suggestions you have
    (D) Any questions if you have and suggestions

about the

decision, please contact our construction office.

13. To wish an actor prior to his going on stage to "break a leg" is a

(A) well-known
(B) well-being
(C) good-known
(D) good-being

practice. A pretty strange wish, actually it is meant magically to bring him luck

14. and make sure

(A) which
(B) what
(C) that
(D) but

his performance will be a success.

15. From the superstitious age,

(A) it was thought
(B) it has been thought
(C) it is thought
(D) it being thought

that jealous forces,

always present, are only too anxious to spoil any venture. A good luck wish would alert

16. and

(A) to provoke them to do
(B) provoke them to do
(C) that provoke them to do
(D) provoked them to do

the evil work,

17.

(A) when
(B) until
(C) while
(D) but

a curse will make them turn their attention elsewhere.

18. The underlying principle is the belief that

(A) that
(B) if
(C) once
(D) but

you wish evil, then good will come. I'm

sure it's called reverse psychology these days.

Questions 19~26 refer to the following article.

19.
| (A) Unlike |
| (B) Like |
| (C) Because |
| (D) If |
photographers on Earth, astronauts have the opportunity to

20. take photographs from unprecedented perspectives.
| (A) Also, |
| (B) Instead, |
| (C) However, |
| (D) Therefore, |
the fairly

21. easy task of taking a photograph on Earth is
| (A) much more |
| (B) more much |
| (C) unless |
| (D) more than |
arduous in space.

22. Zero gravity makes it difficult to stand still, but
| (A) at most |
| (B) at least |
| (C) at ease |
| (D) at once |
it makes it easy to

move heavy camera equipment. On a more fundamental level, the astronauts

23. would find that the spacesuits and other accessories
| (A) worn |
| (B) wearing |
| (C) have been worn |
| (D) have worn |

24. by them
| (A) proving to be |
| (B) prove to be |
| (C) is proven to be |
| (D) have been proven to be |
very cumbersome

25.
(A) when trying
(B) when is trying
(C) when it is tried
(D) it is trying when

to snap the shutter. Other technicalities also make space

photography less than straightforward. For example, photos could be blurred by

26. dirt on windows, and
(A) that is always
(B) it is always
(C) always that is
(D) there is always

the risk of damaging film due to

exposure to just a small amount of radiation.

The largest of the giant gas planets, Jupiter,

27.　with a volume

(A)　greater than 1300 times
(B)　1300 times than greater
(C)　1300 times greater than
(D)　greatest than 1300 times

Earth's, contains more than twice

the mass of all the other planets combined. It is thought to be a gaseous

28.　and fluid planet without solid surfaces.

(A)　It had been
(B)　Had it been
(C)　It is
(D)　There is

somewhat more

29.　massive, Jupiter might have attained internal temperatures

(A)　so high as
(B)　as high as
(C)　so high that
(D)　such high as

the ignition point for nuclear reactions, and it would have flamed as a star in its own right.

Jupiter and the other giant planets are of a low-density type quite

30.

(A)　distinct
(B)　instinct
(C)　distant
(D)　constant

the terrestrial planets:

31.　they

(A)　are composed from
(B)　are composed on
(C)　are composed of
(D)　are composed by

such substances

32.

(A) as
(B) like
(C) unlike
(D) with

hydrogen, helium, ammonia, and methane, unlike terrestrial planets.

Much of Jupiter's interior might be in the form

33. of liquid, metallic hydrogen. Normally, hydrogen is a gas,

(A) but
(B) and
(C) with
(D) without

under

pressures of millions of kilograms per square centimeter,

34.

(A) which exist in the deep interior of Jupiter,
(B) that exist in the deep interior of Jupiter,
(C) of which exist in the deep interior of Jupiter,
(D) exist in which the deep interior of Jupiter,

the hydrogen atoms might

lock together to form a liquid with the properties of a metal.

Questions 35~42 refer to the following article.

35. The basic steps in

(A) make
(B) making
(C) made
(D) having been made

black tea from the raw leaf

are withering, rolling, fermenting, and drying.

36. First the leaves

(A) which are transported from
(B) are transported from
(C) that are transported from
(D) transported from

the plantation to the factory

37.

(A) so rapidly as possible.
(B) as rapidly as possible.
(C) so possible as rapidly.
(D) as possible as rapidly.

The leaves are spread on racks to wither.

38. This removes about

(A) one thirds from
(B) one of thirds
(C) one third of
(D) one third from

the moisture,

39. and the leaves become soft.

(A) Until
(B) Once
(C) After
(D) Since

this they are rolled to

40. break the cells and reduce the juices,

(A) which
(B) that
(C) where
(D) while

are essential for the fermenting

process. Then the leaves are spread out and kept under high humidity

41. to promote fermentation, which

(A) develops
(B) is developing
(C) developed
(D) has developed

the rich flavor of black tea.

42. Then the leaves are dried

(A) since
(B) until
(C) unless
(D) for

the moisture is removed.

Questions 1~4 refer to the following notice.

Dear students,

1.
| (A) Since |
| (B) Because of |
| (C) Due to |
| (D) Although |

the school is going to be on summer vacation, our library will update

the documentation on borrowing books. We strongly require

2. everyone
| (A) to return |
| (B) returning |
| (C) returned |
| (D) return |
all the books you have borrowed before next

3. weekend. In addition, we especially hope you students could check
| (A) whether |
| (B) if |
| (C) that |
| (D) in that |
you

have overdue books or not and return to them in the separate office 303. Tomorrow

4. we will put the namelist of the books
| (A) which is out of shelves |
| (B) that are out of shelves |
| (C) whose are out of shelves |
| (D) what are out of shelves |
on our website.

We are sorry to bring the inconvenience to you.

Questions 5~8 refer to the following announcement.

5.

| (A) Have you noticed that |
| (B) Do you noticing that |
| (C) Have you noticing that |
| (D) Noticed that |

there has been a new statue at the entrance of the teaching

building? Now we want to collect the ideas on naming it. We suggest

6. everyone should

| (A) thinking about |
| (B) think about |
| (C) to think about |
| (D) thought about |

1 to 2 names and then hand in tomorrow.

7. The name must be novel and meaningful.

| (A) In addition, |
| (B) But, |
| (C) Thus, |
| (D) However, |

we need every student

8. to add your reasons

| (A) who |
| (B) what |
| (C) why |
| (D) that |

you want to name it. Detailed description will be

appreciated. Tomorrow afternoon I will come to collect the namelists.

Questions 9~12 refer to the e-mail.

Dear Jason,

I am writing to apologize for breaking our appointment. I cannot go hiking with you this

9. weekend. My cousin and his family just came to

(A) look
(B) watch
(C) see
(D) visit

my family and ask to

10. go out together at the same time.

(A) It has been a long time
(B) Has it been a long time
(C) Long time it been has
(D) Has been it a long time

since I saw him and

11. he will leave next Monday. I really value this chance to

(A) stay with
(B) stay up
(C) stay on
(D) stay off

him. So shall we

postpone our plan to next weekend? I know you have made the preparation for

12. a long time. I am willing to lend my new series of comic books to you

(A) in order to
(B) so as to
(C) so that
(D) that to

you don't need to borrow from bookstores with the limitation of due

time. You can return them whenever you like. Sorry again!

Yours,
Lily

Questions 13~18 refer to the following article from school newspaper.

Every day when I check my e-mail box, there are some letters of students

13.
- (A) complain
- (B) complained
- (C) complaining
- (D) have complained

that writing is too hard.

14. They never write
- (A) unless
- (B) until
- (C) since
- (D) also

assignments require it. They find the writing

15. process really painful. How awful to be able to
- (A) talk
- (B) say
- (C) speak
- (D) tell

in a language but

16. not to write in it,
- (A) especially
- (B) extremely
- (C) particularly
- (D) specially

English, with its rich vocabulary.

17. As a writing teacher, my task is to build fluency
- (A) when
- (B) while
- (C) during
- (D) since

providing the

opportunity inherent in any writing activity to enhance the moral and emotional

18. development of my students. One great way
- (A) to do
- (B) doing
- (C) to doing
- (D) done

this is by having students

write in a journal in class every day. So please begin to write your diaries now!

Questions 19~26 refer to the following article.

The American newspaper is dead! Maybe the reports of the demise of daily journalism

19. are a bit premature. But you cannot open up the newspapers today

(A)	with
(B)	without
(C)	away
(D)	within

20. reading bad news about the papers.

(A)	Declining
(B)	Increasing
(C)	Declined
(D)	Increased

circulation and advertising

21. revenues have forced newsrooms to trim their staffs,

(A)	what
(B)	that
(C)	which
(D)	it

means less real

reporting. A few city papers have closed, while others fill their pages with something

22. valueless or boring. Put simply, it's getting

(A)	so expensive to
(B)	so expensive that
(C)	too expensive to
(D)	too expensive that

gather news.

23. So here's a

(A)	young
(B)	boring
(C)	novel
(D)	old

idea:

24. Let's

(A)	require
(B)	suggest
(C)	get
(D)	make

university professors to do it. For real. And, best of all,

25. free of charge. Remember, most professors aren't paid for

(A)	what
(B)	why
(C)	how
(D)	which

they write

now. When I publish an article in an academic journal, I don't earn a cent. But I

26. also don't engage

(A)	more
(B)	less
(C)	much
(D)	least

than a handful of readers, mainly fellow specialists in my

own field.

Questions 27~34 refer to the article from a magazine.

Thanks to the ubiquity of text on the Internet, we may well be reading more today than

27. we
- (A) did
- (B) done
- (C) doing
- (D) do

in the past. But it's a different kind of reading, and behind it

28.
- (A) lies
- (B) lays
- (C) lying
- (D) laying

a different kind of thinking—perhaps even a new sense of the self.

29. "We are not only
- (A) who
- (B) which
- (C) what
- (D) how

we read," says Maryanne Wolf, a developmental

30. psychologist in Tufts University. "We are how we read." Wolf
- (A) worries about
- (B) worried about
- (C) worries that
- (D) worried that

31. the style
- (A) of
- (B) in
- (C) on
- (D) over

reading promoted be the Net, a style that puts "efficiency" and

"immediacy" above all else, maybe weakening our capacity for the kind of deep reading

32. that
- (A) emerged
- (B) merged
- (C) immerged
- (D) submerged

when an earlier technology, the printing press, made long and

complex works of prose commonplace. When we read online, she says,

33. we tend

(A) in
(B) to
(C) on
(D) of

become "mere decoders of information". Our ability to interpret

text, to make the rich mental connections that form when we read deeply and without

34. distraction,

(A) remain
(B) remains
(C) remained
(D) remaining

largely disengaged.

35. When you are trying to make a good impression,

(A) that is saying it
(B) it is said that
(C) that is to say
(D) it is that said

you should

36. put your "best foot forward". There are many options

(A) so as to
(B) so to
(C) as to
(D) as so to

where this phrase

37. came from, one being that it was believed

(A) that
(B) which
(C) what
(D) how

"the left" was the realm of the

Devil, of evil and misfortune. After all the Latin word sinister means left, and in

38. English sinister has kept its ominous meaning.

(A) Hence,
(B) Because,
(C) Besides,
(D) However,

it was advisable to

keep the left foot behind and step forward with the best, the right, foot first. But this

39. phrase seems to have come from the fashion world, rather than

(A) anything
(B) something
(C) everything
(D) nothing

40. mysterious. The saying can

(A) be traced to
(B) date back
(C) be dated to
(D) trace back

male vanity, particularly apparent in the

late eighteenth century, the period of the dandy. The desire to attract people's attention and

admiration took strange and elaborate forms. At the time, people

41.   imagined that their two legs

(A) differed
(B) differing
(C) different
(D) differentiate

in shape and that "normally" one was

more becoming than the other. To draw attention to it they

42.   kept the

(A) bad
(B) worse
(C) good
(D) better

one in the background, literally putting "their best foot forward",

and with it, of course, their leg.

Answers & Explanations

1. C 句子理解为"Mr. Philip 告诉了我这件事，并且让我帮助你制订详细的安排"。固定搭配：ask sb. to do sth. "请某人做某事"。

2. A set out 表示"动身，启程，出发"。

3. C if 引导虚拟语气，句子可理解为"如果你能联系我并告知你的计划的话，我会很感激"。

4. B so that 引导目的状语，"你把你的计划告诉了我，我就能在下周三之前作出计划报告"，so that 和 in order to 都表示"为了……"，in order to 后面加动词原形，so that 后面加句子。

5. A since 表示"因为"，引导原因状语从句。because of 也有"因为"的意思，但是后面不能跟句子。

6. B 句子理解为"每个人都可以随意写，例如降价、增加特色小吃、设置自动售货机等等"。anything 表示"任何事情"。

7. D there be 句型表示"某处有某物"。

8. A 学校正在收集 ideas or suggestions，应该用进行时 looking forward to。

9. A The reason 为全句主语，is 为谓语，选项部分为修饰 reason 的定语，动词应选用非谓语形式，排除选项 C 和 D。reason 是被给出的，因此选择被动形式 given。

10. C 免费校车被取消，逻辑上应该是很少有学生或是没有学生乘坐。few 和 little 都表示"很少的"，few 修饰可数名词，little 修饰不可数名词。students 为可数名词，因此选择 few。

11. C neighborhoods 表示"邻近地区"，是环绕在校园周边，主动形式用 surrounding。

12. A 选项的意思可被理解为"如果你有任何问题或建议"，用正常语序，由 if 引导。

13. A well-known 为形容词，表示"众所周知的，著名的"。

14. C 此句为宾语从句，选项后面的 his performance will be a success 成分及内容完整，可选择 that。此处 that 无实义，且不充当成分。

15. C it is thought that... 表示"据认为……"，题目理解为"从有迷信观念的时代开始，人们就认为无时不在的嫉妒心会使人焦虑不已，从而毁掉一切机会"。

16. B and 为并列连词，并列两个分句，前后两个动词应该是形态一致，alert 为动词原形，provoke 也应该为动词原形。

17. C "一个好的祝愿会提醒和激发嫉妒心施展邪恶的伎俩，但一个诅咒却能将它们的注意力转移到别处。"while 表示转折和对比关系。

18. B "如果你期待厄运的话，好运往往会降临。"if 表示"如果"，从句是现在时态，主句要用将来时态。

19. A 句子理解为"和地球上的摄影师不同的是，宇航员有机会以前所未有的视角拍摄照片"。unlike 表示"和……不同"。

20. C　easy 表示"容易的"，和后面的 arduous 构成对比，有转折关系，故选择 however。

21. A　比较费力，用 much more arduous。

22. B　句子理解为"零重力会使站直变成比较困难的事情，但至少移动沉重的照相设备还是比较容易的"。at least 表示"至少"；at most 表示"至多，不超过"；at ease 表示"安逸，不拘束"；at once 表示"立刻，马上"。

23. A　the spacesuits and other accessories（太空服和其他装饰品）是被穿在宇航员身上的，排除选项 B。非谓语动词可以修饰名词，所以要选择 worn。

24. B　"穿在宇航员身上的太空服和其他装饰品被证明是非常笨重的，尤其是当宇航员试图快速按下照相机快门的时候"，prove 为谓语动词，主动时态不用被动形式。

25. A　当主句和从句的主语相同或指代同一事物时，且从句中有 be 动词，可以省略从句中的主语和 be 动词。

26. D　there is 表示"某处有某物"，句子理解为"因为暴露在少量的辐射下，胶卷可能有被破坏的风险"。

27. C　"比……大几倍"用"倍数 + greater than"。

28. B　had it been somewhat more massive = if it had been somewhat more massive，意思是"如果木星再稍微大一些的话，其内部温度就会跟核反应堆的燃点一样高"，是虚拟语气。

29. B　"和……一样高"用 as high as。

30. A　通过后一句的 unlike 推断前面应该是 distinct，表示"和……不同"。

31. C　be composed of 表示"由……组成"。

32. A　such... as 表示"像……一样的"。

33. A　句子理解为"通常情况下，氢气是种气体，但是在每平方厘米所承受的成千上万的压力之下，氢原子会连锁形成有金属性能的液体"，前后对比用 but。

34. A　选项用来修饰 pressures，为非限定性定语从句，所以用 which。

35. B　in 为介词，后面要加 ing 形式。

36. B　叶子是从种植园运到工厂去的，所以用被动语态。

37. B　as...as possible 表示"尽可能的……"。

38. C　one third 表示"三分之一"，"……的"用介词 of 表示。

39. C　"在叶子被取出三分之一的湿度后，他们被碾破细胞，减少汁水，这是使它们发酵的重要一步"，after 表示"在……之后"。

40. A　非限定性定语从句，用 which。

41. A　which 指代前半句话，动词用第三人称单数形式。

42. B　句子理解为"直到湿气完全被除去，叶子才变干了"。

Practice Set 2

1. A 句子理解为"由于学校要放暑假了"，since 引导原因状语从句，语气较弱，表示已知的原因，常译为"由于；既然"。

2. D require sb. (should) do sth. 意为"要求某人做某事"，return books 表示"还书"。

3. A whether 可以和 or not 连用，表示"是否"。

4. B 选项部分为修饰 books 的定语从句，选项 C 和 D 的连接词不对，books 是复数，选项 A 不对。

5. A 句子理解为"你是否已经注意到了教学楼前的新雕塑呢？"注意要用完成时态。

6. B suggest sb. (should) do sth. 表示"建议某人做某事"。

7. A in addition 表示"此外，还有"；but 和 however 都表示"但是"，but 后面不能加逗号；thus 表示"所以"。

8. C reasons 后面跟 why，why you want to name it 是用来修饰 reasons 的。

9. D visit 表示"拜访"。

10. A 正常语序，it has been a long time 表示"有很长一段时间了"，是现在完成时。

11. A stay with 表示"与某人待在一起"；stay up 表示"熬夜"；stay on 表示"保持"；stay off 表示"远离"。

12. C in order to 和 so that 都表示"为了"，in order to 后面要跟动词原形，so that 后面跟句子。

13. C complaining 表示学生主动抱怨。

14. A 句子理解为"他们从来不写作，除非有作业这样要求"。unless 表示"除非"。

15. C 句子理解为"能说一门语言，但是不能用这种语言写作是多么糟糕啊"，表示"说一门语言"要用 speak。

16. A especially 表示"尤其是"，这里特指英语。

17. B while 表示"同时"。

18. A 不定式 to do 表示要做的。

19. B 句子理解为"翻开今天的报纸，你不会看不到坏消息"，without 表示"没有"。

20. A 句子理解为"正在下降的发行量和广告收入已经迫使发行商裁减员工"。这里是动名词作主语。

21. C which 引导的非限定性定语从句。

22. C too...to... 结构表示"太……而不能……"。

23. C novel 表示"新颖的"。

24. C get sb. to do sth. 表示"让某人做某事"，require，suggest 和 make 后面要加 do。

25. A what 引导的宾语从句，句子理解为"现在大部分教授不是以写东西来赚钱的"。

26. A not more than 表示"不多于"。

27. A in the past 表示过去时态，动词用过去式。